The Ballad Mongers

OTHER BOOKS BY OSCAR BRAND

Bawdy Songs and Backroom Ballads (Ed.)

Singing Holidays: The Calendar in Folk Song

Folk Songs for Fun

How to Play Folk Songs

The

rise of the modern

Funk & Wagnalls Company, Inc.   New York

OSCAR BRAND

BALLAD MONGERS

folk song

Acknowledgments:

I am grateful to the publishers of the following songs for their graciousness in allowing me to use their material.

FROGG New words and new music arranged by Dick Foley, Bob Flick, Mike Kirkland, and John Paine. Copyright 1961 Bigareff Music, Inc., New York, N. Y. Used by permission.

IF I HAD A HAMMER (The Hammer Song) and WASN'T THAT A TIME Words and Music by Lee Hays and Pete Seeger. Copyright 1958 and 1960 Ludlow Music, Inc., New York, N. Y. Used by permission.

UNION MAID Words and Music by Woody Guthrie. Copyright 1961 Ludlow Music, Inc., New York, N. Y. Used by permission.

A GUY IS A GUY Words and Music by Oscar Brand. Copyright 1952 and 1961 Ludlow Music, Inc., New York, N. Y. Used by permission.

ROUND AND ROUND HITLER'S GRAVE Used by permission of the Guthrie Children's Trust Fund.

WHICH SIDE ARE YOU ON? By Florence Reece. Copyright 1946 by People's Songs Inc. Used by permission of *Sing Out* magazine.

NINETY CENTS BUTTER By The Almanac Singers. Copyright 1946 by People's Songs Inc. Used by permission.

SIXTEEN TONS By Merle Travis. Copyright 1947 by American Music, Inc., Hollywood, California. Used by special permission.

To my sister, Edythe, and my brother, Harry

Preface

This book is a very personalized and subjective appraisal of an important segment of my world. I learned folk music as a child in Canada, and acquired a large pack of songs in my travels about the United States. In those years I never thought to inquire into the significance and historical perspective provided by the songs—I simply enjoyed their company.

In 1945, I left the United States Army and began to sing professionally. I even learned to play a guitar in order to cover my vocal deficiencies. Then I had to learn special songs for special occasions—broadcasts, pageants, rallies. I swapped information with pedants, professors, and players. In a few years I was an expert. All sorts of people began coming to me for misinformation.

Years went by. Women with grown daughters came by

to tell me how they had heard me sing in their own childhood days, or had sung with me the militant songs of 1938. I was becoming a "dean." Before I become a "legend," I want to tell today's story—to defer the moment when I must gloss over the unpleasant memories to fit my own exalted image.

I want to remember further that it was Herbert Katz who first suggested this book, and Arnold Andersen who made me finish it. There are others who come to mind and are herein noted, neither in alphabetical order nor in order of importance: Evelyn Singer, Fred Hellerman, Peter Kameron, Al Brackman, Einar Savig, Ed Cramer, Theodora Zavin, and Julie Newman.

And, of course, I mustn't forget to thank Agnes De Mille, for consenting to add her own appraisal of the world of folk music.

O. B.

New York, July 1, 1962

Foreword

At this moment when America finds herself, quite to the amazement of all, the most powerful of contemporary nations and very possibly the most influential, it is imperative that exact stock be taken of her nature and worth. All people are studying the American character and the American point of view with a compulsion born of anxiety, resentment, or fear; born of hope, of gratitude, and even, in some instances, of admiration. In the light of such universal appraisal we ourselves are forced into a similar re-evaluation. "Who are we?" we ask, "and what do we want?" And we ask with the whole world. We must answer truthfully, because very likely the fate of the world depends on our findings.

Where can we look for instruction? In business figures? In statistics of population growth? of education? of careers and professions? In the personalities of our best-known citizens?

Not in any of these, nor in all of them together. Not even in political or public activities, for people on occasion can be misled; on occasion they badly fail their intent. We must search out more intimate clues, the thumb-prints of the individual life, the earth-castings of the generations. It is in daily ways that people reveal themselves: in manners and habits, in the jokes they laugh at, the steps they dance, the tunes and words they sing. Folk songs, therefore, mirror most closely the will and essence of any group, not, to be sure, the great art songs which of their nature are unique, but the lesser and more homely ballads which are typical and which, because they reflect pervasive and common emotion, are remembered and kept. Here we come face to face with Anon. And he turns out to be quite a person; he turns out to be us.

These songs constitute history but are not subject to the selectivity or discrimination of the historian. They escape the editing of sophisticated taste or the censorship or the curbing of interested taste. And while certain sublime rousers like "Bonnie Dundee," "The Marseillaise," or "The Battle Hymn of the Republic" have had noticeably stirring effect, it must always be borne in mind that this effect was spontaneous, that it could not be contrived, and that regardless of sponsorship no folk song ever is successful when it does not suit the prevailing need. It is the answer to a situation, not the cause of it. For this reason it can be said that while propaganda incites, folk poetry recites. It does not, however, recite impartially. Folk poetry is partial. It has to do with *now*—how it feels at the moment while the blood is still fresh, while the wind still blows and the calls ring out. No dust ever settles in a folk song.

Economy is the great hallmark, suggestion and dramatic impact the essence of the business. Except curiously in America, for reasons explained in the book, the weak, the sentimental, the paltry has never been retained. What has passed down to us usually has been stark and effective, regardless of mood.

Everyone who is concerned with folk singing, and that means all of us whether or not we are aware of the fact, will find a wealth of provocative material here. Oscar Brand gives examples of delicious and little-known songs and remarkable variations and transmutations of staples, sorting out the interweaving strains and creative impulses of our cultural development. Interested amateurs will find tantalizing new leads; the general reader will be instructed in much that concerns him—the long and poignant history behind all our singing, our mottos, our jingles and nursery rhymes. Who will again, after reading page 23, repeat "Little Jack Horner" carelessly, without a shudder at human venality, without wonder at human resilience and irony? Here indeed green moss grows on gallows bones.

He will be instructed in those deviations from cultural patterns peculiarly American: the emerging of the spontaneous folk cry with big business and the resulting distortion and corruption of public taste and the medium itself, the unchanging phenomenon of elaborate tireless quarreling between the purists and those exuberant performers who believe that the songs are there for the singing in any manner and vernacular that suits. Of course there is the matter of taste; one day there will be a great winnowing out, and only original forms will stand, simply because they are the strongest and the most pungent. In the meantime, anyone can compose his own folk variants and sing them as he pleases. And why not? He has just as much right to be anonymous as anyone else. And out of the rich and indigenous mulch of this unschooled experimental warbling come many surprising and brilliant devices, and, on occasion, even poetry and a tune.

We are at present engulfed in a tidal wave of folk singing. It is the largest and most profitable do-it-yourself fad since the western land rushes. Our modest and hitherto nameless troubadour finds himself today a national influence with a name that pays millions. The curious tale is here spelled out meticulously: the early exploration, scholarly or otherwise, the first tentative recognition, the vogue, the capturing, perversion, and martyrdom of talent, the present great power with its predicaments and perils. This book adds a revealing chapter to our social and cultural history, and should be of inestimable help to those who wish to study not only the various folk forms but the facts behind their creating. They are worth considering. For if our folk singers are "the abstracts and brief chronicle of the time," it were wise to use them well. As Hamlet suggests, ". . . after your death you were better have a bad epitaph than their ill report while you live." They are not to be muzzled or tampered with. They must be heard as they wish to be heard, for our own sake as well as theirs. It is our report, our only epitaph, that we, through our meddling, are about to deface.

AGNES DE MILLE

Merriewold, 1962

Contents

The Ballad Mongers

1.

The Simple Noise

One of America's leading popular song publishers instructed a contract songwriter, "Bring in a tune that doesn't have to be composed." The head of one of our leading record firms made a general appeal for "songs that don't need more than three chords for accompaniment." They were both referring to the same need, resulting from the sudden interest of the American public in folk music and folk-type songs.

This resurgence of folk song in America is not restricted to the "Hit Parade." It is evident in our serious music, in motion picture scores, in the background music for television and radio drama, in our school curriculum, and, as always, in our children's games and general social singing. Those who insist that they will hold no truck with folk music are to be pitied. As the old spiritual has it, "There is no hiding place down here."

What is this "folk song" which has reinsinuated itself into national popularity? How has it been able to attain such great acceptance? What factors in our national life have helped bring the resurgence about? Who is in the vanguard of this movement? What promise does the future hold for the folk music fan? In seeking to answer these questions, we are handicapped by the fact that few experts agree even upon the simple definition of a folk song.

In 1953 Duncan Emrich, then Curator of the Folksong Archives of the Library of Congress, commented in a letter to the *Saturday Review*, "The theory of 'communal creation' of the ballads has been thoroughly exploded for several decades. At its point of origin, each folk song is the creation of an individual."

Yet, not everyone has completely relinquished the belief that a folk song has no author. I have been reintroduced to this theory many times by members of audiences from the Golden Gate to the George Washington Bridge. I wasn't surprised when a well-known moderator on a CBS television broadcast explained to the audience that the song I had just sung wasn't really a folk song because the name of the author was to be found in the last verse:

This song it was made by Billy Gashade
  As soon as the news did arrive.
He said there was no man with the law in his hand
  Could take Jesse James when alive.

The moderator assumed that, since Billy Gashade was not a community, the product of his genius was not really a folk song.

Another belief which has not been easily surrendered by the general public is the "vulgar origin of folk music." This early hypothesis had certain advantages. If it could be assumed that the folk song was the product of illiterate poets without musical training, it would follow that the listener would probably reproduce the song improperly. The next "peasant" would then alter the song even more. After the song had been subjected to enough imperfections, the product, the result of "community error," would be eligible for the title "folk song."

However, accredited folk songs exist whose original creators were college professors, medical doctors, serious-music composers, and high government officials. The original authorship is not the test at all. According to the International Folk Music Council, to merit the title, a folk song has to have weathered the "process of oral transmission: it is the product of evolution, and is dependent on the circumstances of continuity, variation, and selection." In other words, the important factor is "Where did the song go after the moment of composition?"

One of our earliest folk songs is "The Yankee's Return from Camp." It has been described as derived from "an anti-Cromwell jingle," "an aria from a seventeenth-century opera," "a Dutch laborers' song," and "a Spanish children's game." It is generally accepted, however, that the song we know now as "Yankee Doodle" was a composition by Dr. Richard Shuckburgh, a British army medical officer. Dr. Shuckburgh was making fun of the ragged, unmilitary colonial militia, but soon those same militiamen were rewriting the song into a stirring revolutionary anthem. And most Americans today agree with the 1800 lyric:

Oh, Yankee Doodle is the tune,
   Americans delight in,
'Twill do to whistle, sing, or play,
   And just the thing for fightin'.

"Yankee Doodle" meets the test of oral transmission, continuity, variation, and selection. It is widely accepted as a folk song.

In 1863, Henry C. Work composed an antislavery song, "The Year of Jubilo."

Oh, darkies, have you seen the massa,
   Wif de mustache on his face,
Gwine down the road dis very ebening
   Like he's gwine to leab dis place?
He heard the noise from down the ribber,
   Where de Linkum gunboats lay,
He grab his coat and he left very sudden,
   And I specs he's run away.

Since Composer Work had already produced "Grandfather's Clock," "Nicodemus Awake," and "Marching through Georgia," it was assumed that the new song would meet with public approval. The sheet music was purchased by thousands of pianists and the song was sung and resung throughout the Northern states. At this point in its career, it was just another art song, al-

though superior to most. But soon the soldiery took up
the song without recourse to the printed lyric or music.
The words were altered, as is usually true where transmission depends on the vagaries of human recollection.
Recently, in the South, I heard this version of the old
song:

Oh, fellows, have you seen Uncle Riley,
    With the mustache on his face?
He spied a coon dis very morning,
    And he chased it round the place.

This contemporary version of "The Year of Jubilo" meets
with all the above-mentioned requirements. Henry C.
Work may be credited with having originated a folk
song.

So far, the International Music Council seems to have
answered many of the questions which plague the for-
agers in the field of folk music. But suddenly we are
moved to inquire, "At which point does the song become
a folk song?" "How many changes and transfers are
necessary?" Some experts prefer twenty as a key number. A few will accept ten, if these provide enough
variation. One or two will accept five versions, if the
time span is over fifty years. Actually, while these figures are not really proposed seriously, contemporary articles in folklore journals often imply such reliance on
numerology.

When does a musical creation merit the title "folk
song"? Many folklorists answer this question by rely-
ing on their political orientation. Protest songs have
always been a source of controversy in folk music cir-

cles. Take "Joe Hill" as an example. We know the name of the author, Alfred Hayes, as well as that of the composer, Earl Robinson. We have available sheet music. The song is heard now in many variations, it is true, but those who accept these as folk music are usually liberal and labor-vectored, while an expert who calls the song "prevarication in maudlin doggerel," is generally conservative in his social attitudes.

An early American song, "Redwing," was converted into a bawdy ballad during the late nineteenth century. More recently, Woodrow Wilson Guthrie, whom Alan Lomax has called "America's greatest living ballad-writer," rewrote "Redwing" into a labor anthem, "The Union Maid":

There once was a union maid
Who never was afraid
Of goons, and ginks, and company finks,
And the deputy sheriffs who made the raid;
She'd go to a union hall,
When a meeting it was called,
And when the company boys came around,
She always stood her ground.

A folk song authority with many books and public-service awards to his credit immediately hailed the song as a true expression of the American people and a fine folk song. Other similar efforts, including "The Union Casey Jones," "Listen, Mr. Bigot," and "Ninety Cents Butter and Ninety Cents Meat (How in the world can a poor man eat)," were accepted as bona-finds by the same expert.

A short time ago, I learned an antiunion miners' song

which had been created in Southern Illinois from a re-write of a mountaineer lullaby:

Come and listen to my song,
Story of a nation wronged,
Gangsters in a roving band,
Struck the tools from a miner's hand.
Flag of blue, white and red,
Man's got a right to earn his bread.

Some of the verses were very moving, and, despite my own union affiliations and sympathy, I repeated the song for the aforementioned folk song authority. "That's not really a folk song," he said. "Only a scab would sing it." Applying his own standard of "Not in the public interest," he rejected the new creation as "unfolksong-like."

A. L. Lloyd, one of England's foremost authorities, has written, "English folk song is something that came out of social upheaval. . . . It grew up with a class just establishing itself in society. . . . When that class declined, the folk song withered away and died." Nevertheless, A. L. Lloyd, who is a remarkably fine performer, includes in his own repertory many industrial ballads and political songs of relatively recent composition. His singing companion, Ewan MacColl, prints in his excellent collections of Scottish folk music many compositions of his own making. In sum, for many experts, a song may be accredited as "a folk song" if it meets with a specific need of the working classes. With other experts, a hint of a propaganda element is enough to invalidate a large part of our songbag. For that reason, it is wise to continually reexamine the bias of the particular expert on whose judgment we rely for the definition of "a folk song."

At this point, I should explain my own bias so that you can evaluate my references throughout this book. When I refer to "traditional song," I am applying the definition promulgated by the International Folk Music Council, "Music that has been submitted to the process of oral transmission: It is the product of evolution, and is dependent on the circumstances of continuity, variation, and selection." The one hundred variations of "Barbara Allen" in the archives of the Congressional Library meet with these requirements. And, until the moment when The Weavers sang "On Top of Old Smoky" on to the Top Ten, the many versions of the song were "traditional."

Sometimes, however, I refer to as "a folk song" a song which does not meet with all the elements of the Council's definition. That is because I use a very subjective rule of thumb in selecting my folk songbag. And, since it *is* subjective, it cannot suit anyone but me, and will rarely satisfy anyone else. Nevertheless, as far as I am concerned, a folk song is distinguishable by a special sound, a kind of "simple noise." This sound is the result of an artless, unself-conscious quality in the music and lyrics which commends itself to my critical ear. I can usually recognize this simplicity when I meet it in American and Canadian song, but I find myself less sure when I encounter the folk music of foreign lands. I can humbly confess that most Chinese songs sound alike to me. And the difference between a Kirghiz art song and a Kirghiz folk song is beyond my comprehension. Consequently, for the most part, I shall use my definition only when discussing North American music.

This simple sound is sometimes characteristic of modern songs such as "Casey Jones." On April 20, 1901, engineer Jones, nicknamed "Casey" for the little town of Cayce, Kentucky, in which he was born, was killed in a train wreck. Wiper Wallace Saunders rewrote an old railroader's song to describe the fatal accident. The Leighton Brothers, a well-known vaudeville act, rewrote the song and sang it into national popularity. A Shapiro-Bernstein copyright will protect their interests until 1965. Despite the printed words and music, I call "Casey Jones" a folk song, because it has the "simple noise" which is my measuring stick.

Another example is the song "Happy Birthday." This was originally written by the two Hill Sisters as part of a children's music play. America desperately needed a birthday song and the original words, "Good morning to you" were changed and sung around the nation in their new form. The sisters derived considerable satisfaction and royalties whenever a telegraph boy sang their song on a strange doorstep—until a few years ago when the copyright expired. Despite this well-known and easy-to-chart background, I'd accept "Happy Birthday" as a folk song.

John Jacob Niles is an accomplished composer from Boot Hill, Kentucky, now busily at work on a symphony. One day, many years ago, he heard a short poem recited by a little mountain girl. He wrote some additional verses, composed a haunting melody, and published the work as "I Wonder as I Wander." Many authorities include this work in the folk song catalogue because they are unaware of its origin. I would include this work in the charmed circle because it has the "simple sound" I love. Others of Niles' creations would probably be acceptable as well, among them, "Venezuela," "The Lass from the Low Country," and the music for the best-known version of "Black is the Color of My True Love's Hair."

In like manner, I shall feel free to call "Free America" a folk song, although I know it was written by General Joseph Warren a few days before his valiant death at Bunker Hill:

Lift up your heads, ye heroes,
   And swear with proud disdain
The wretch that would ensnare you
   Shall lay his snares in vain.
Let Europe empty all her force,
   We'll meet her in array,
Huzzah, huzzah, huzzah,
   For a free Amerikay.

I shall call "The Big Rock Candy Mountain" a folk song, although I know it was written by Mac McClintock, and that the popular version was rewritten by Burl Ives. And I will not exclude "The Frozen Logger" merely because it was created by Stewart Holbrook, James Stevens, and H. L. Davis for a 1929 radio broadcast. I mention these in order to make clear that many folk music experts would not accept my catalogue of "folk songs." Therefore, I shall, wherever possible, describe the history of the songs I use for examples, and cite the scholarly authorities with whom I disagree.

I have one other category which needs immediate defining, "The Folk-Type Song." Into this pigeonhole I consign the many songs of folk origin which sound slightly self-conscious and overblown. An example is "Fair and Free Elections," which has been traced back to 1848:

> While some on rights and some on wrongs,
>   Prefer their own reflections,
> The people's right must still be strong,
>   The right to free elections.
> Should enemies beset our land,
>   With traitor's disaffections,
> Undaunted, we will stand our ground,
>   Upheld by free elections.

The sentiment is commendable, and the melody is "Yankee Doodle," but I would list this as a folk-type song.

Many art songs strive for the "simple noise," but fall short. The lyric "Scarlet Ribbons" is one. "Spanish Is the Loving Tongue" is another. And, at the risk of being accused of striking at the cornerstone of American democracy, I would list "Home on the Range" as another. "My Western Home," as it was originally called, was written in 1873 by Dr. Brewster Higley, a pioneer who practiced his medical art on the windswept Kansas plain. The music was supplied by his neighbor, Daniel E. Kelley. The song was transmitted orally all over our land, and there are hundreds of variations. Despite the

beautiful melody, however, it is hard to believe in the
mildly banal lyric,

Oh, give me a land where the bright diamond sand,
  Flows leisurely down the stream,
Where the graceful white swan goes gliding along
  Like a maid in a heavenly dream.

In the category of "folk-type songs," I shall also include the thousands of published pieces listed in music
catalogues as "Hillbilly and Western." Some of them are
based on traditional airs, and may even use verses from
the old ballads, but, usually, the faltering hand of the
modern rewrite man changes the material enough to
warrant exclusion from the list of folk songs.

You will see, therefore, that each song must be examined individually for that special ring of truth which I
feel is germane to the folk song. The works of Stephen
Foster are, with few exceptions, "folk-type songs." But
I would recommend "Oh, Susannah," and "The Glendy
Burke" for any folk song program. The hundreds of
songs by Robert Burns present another problem, a very
knotty one. It's easy to say that the lyric of his "The Deil
Tak to the Wars" is not a folk song:

Sleep'st thou, or wak'st thou, fairest creature?
  Rosy Morn now lifts his eye,
Numbering ilka bud which Nature
  Waters wi' the tears o' joy.

And I stand with a million others to acclaim "Coming
through the Rye" as a genuine folk song. But then we

come to the verses Burns wrote to the tune of "The Yellow-haired Laddie," the song he called "Flow Gently, Sweet Afton." For two verses, this beautiful air has the folk song quality. Then he waxes ultrapoetic:

Thy crystal stream, Afton, how lovely it glides,
And winds by the cot where my Mary resides.
How wanton thy waters her snowy feet lave,
As gathering sweet flowerets she stems thy clear wave.

In categorizing "Flow Gently, Sweet Afton," I would say that, in part, it has the qualities of a folk song, and, in part, it is the product of a slightly self-conscious poet.

We all enjoy singing Burns' and Stephen Foster's lively and often beautiful songs. However, I am not now trying to judge their musical worth. I am merely attempting to show the standards by which I judge the "folk song" and the "folk-type song." Each must be examined for simplicity, down-to-earth plain talk, and the ring of truth. It may be a ballad that tells of ancient lords and their ladies, but they must be real people under the finery. It may be a song that conflicts with our political beliefs, if it is earnest and honest. It may be a tree-high tall tale, so long as it flows from the wellsprings of our common humanity.

In other words, the "folk song" should have the characteristics of most of our "traditional" songs, from which the unreal, the phony, and the unnecessary have been worn away by the processes of oral transmission and the passage of time. The "folk song" may be a thousand years old, or may have been written yesterday by

Woody Guthrie and Huddie Ledbetter. It may be two thirds of Robert Burns' songs, or one tenth of the compositions of Stephen Foster. In any case, these will be the standards by which I list the songs we shall presently meet.

2.

London Bridge

One of the questions most frequently asked of any folk singer is, "When did you first become interested in folk music?" For many, the interest began when folk music appeared in quantity on the Hit Parade. But we must remember that during childhood all Americans are folk singers. Usually, the child learns his first folk song from his mother, who painstakingly forces his little hands together and pulls them apart while singing:

Patacake, patacake, baker's man,
Bake me a cake whenever you can,
Make it and bake it and mark it with a P,
And put it in the oven for baby and me.

The "marking it with a P" section is the most fun because mother usually draws a "P" with her finger on baby's stomach.

Soon the child will also be exposed to "Eensie Beensie Spider" and "Rockabye, Baby." When he is older and more malleable, he will be taught to sing and dance to "All Around the Mulberry Bush," "London Bridge," and "The Farmer in the Dell."

The parent cannot handle this tremendous task alone. Children also learn these age-old games and songs from their playmates. Before long, each one of us is packed full of traditional material which would last a lifetime were it not for the stultifying effect of the mass media. Of course, nowadays, with the high incidence of folk song on the popular song parade, it seems as if our whole culture is devoted to the reproduction of folk music.

The first song a child hears is the lullaby, and, consequently, lullabies are the first songs that children learn. The lullaby usually is based on a simple formula used to lull the child to sleep: Mommy is here. Mommy loves you. Nothing will harm you. If you go to sleep, Mommy will reward you. The earliest known lullaby doesn't bother with even these promises. It just goes, "La, la, la la." An early Roman fragment has been found which is slightly more eloquent:

Lalla, lalla, lalla,
Aut dormi, aut lacte.

The words, freely translated, mean "Either sleep or drink your milk." By 1398, John De Trevisa wrote that

"Nouryces vse lullynges and other cradyl songes to pleyse the wyttes of the chylde." In 1372, one lullaby is noted as entreating, "Softe slep and faste," and in the fifteenth century the Christmas pageant of the Shearmen and Tailors featured a lullaby ascribed to the women of Bethlehem just before Herod's soldiers appeared to kill their children:

Lully, lullay, thou little tiny child,
    By by, lully lullay,
Herod, the king, in his raging,
    Chargèd he hath this day,
His men of might, in his own sight,
    All young children to slay.

Except for "Hush, Little Baby, Don't Say a Word," few lullabies have been successfully exploited outside the nursery. But this doesn't mean that our ballad mongers have ignored the possibility. For instance, there is the antiunion song mentioned on page 9, which was originally a lullaby:

What shall we do with the baby-o?
What shall we do with the baby-o?
What shall we do with the baby-o?
Wrap him up in calico.
Eyes of blue, cheeks of red,
Lips as sweet as gingerbread.

According to Fleming Brown of Chicago, the nonunion miners sang:

Flag of blue, white and red,
Man's got a right to earn his bread.

John L's pay is big and fat;
Wish I had one tenth of that.
Man's got a right to dig for coal;
Man's got a right to own his soul.

Many of the songs of childhood are originals, written and produced by the children themselves. Among the documents in the Archives of American Song in the Library of Congress is a pile of contributions printed on lined paper with red, blue, and yellow crayon. These are songs and games submitted by correspondents who usually observe before their signatures, "Nine years old," or "I am six." One little girl warns, "I am only four." City and country children in every land have in common the simple four-note chant used for such ditties as "Brass buttons, blue coat, couldn't catch a nanny-goat," or "Fat, Fat, the water rat, fifty bullets in his hat." These are found in abundance in the aforementioned pile.

The children also compose chants for their games and street choruses, and many of these contain lines derived from popular songs, from motion picture titles, and from newspaper headlines:

Good King Wenceslas walked out,
In his mother's garden,
Bumped into a Brussels sprout,
And said, "I beg your pardon."

One, two, three, four,
Charlie Chaplin went to war.
When the Hun began to fight,
Charlie Chaplin said, "Goodnight."

Children can derive their songs and chants from other odd sources such as advertising slogans and political campaign catchwords:

Tippecanoe and Tyler, too,
Three, four, five, six . . . etc.

In the early days, in England, it was necessary for the children to adopt adult material for their purposes, because no one bothered to create songs for the small singers. The general attitude was that children were merely "small adults," as is evidenced by the seventeenth-century paintings showing children as miniature grownups. Consequently, the contemporary child's garden of verses is replete with remnants of old bawdy songs, political satires, and echoes of tavern glees.

Only the Jews bothered with songs specially constructed for the use of children, and two of these led to a fascinating progression. The service for the second night of Passover ends with two chants, the first of which asks:

Who knoweth thirteen?
I, saith Israel, know thirteen:
Thirteen divine attributes, twelve tribes, eleven stars,
Ten commandments, nine months before childbirth,
Eight days before circumcision, seven days in the week,
Six books of the Mishnah, five books of the law,
Four matrons, three patriarchs, two tables of covenant,
But one is God alone which is over heaven and earth.

It is generally accepted that this "Ehod Mi Yode'a'" was parodied by the British to make the cumulative song "Green Grow the Rushes-O":

I'll sing you one-o, green grow the rushes-o.
What is your one-o? Green grow the rushes-o.
One is one and all alone and ever more shall be so.

Further development of the song in America turned it into a chain-gang song called, "Holy Babe":

Children, go where I send thee,
How shall I send thee?
I'm a-going to send thee one by one,
One for the little bitty baby,
Wrapped in swaddling clothing,
Laying in the manger,
Born, born, born in Bethlehem.

The second Passover chant, "Had Gadyo," also had an interesting historical development. During the Passover service, the child delighted in the mystic words:

Then came the Most Holy, blessed be He,
And slew the slaughterer who had slaughtered the ox,
Which had drunk the water which had burnt the staff,
Which had smitten the dog which had bitten the cat,
Which had eaten the kid my father had bought for two
    zuzim,
Only one kid, one kid.

According to the interpreters of Hebrew chants, the cat represents Babylon, the dog represents Persia, and so on. But the children didn't care what the dog represented; they just enjoyed the chant. And, in early England, British children used a similar refrain, "This is the House That Jack Built."

Since it is agreed that, with the above exceptions, few songs were especially constructed for children before the eighteenth century, scholars are always examining the very old songs for secret adult meanings. Early pagan rituals are to be found in "All Around the Mulberry Bush" (Druidic incantation), "London Bridge" (immuring of live sacrifices), and "Ladybird, Ladybird" (divination using the friendly little insect known as "Our Lady's Bird" which can also exorcise evil spirits). Even "Billy Boy" has been traced to the older, more poignant ballad, "Lord Randall."

In order to shed light on obscure moments in history, scholars have been carefully examining the songs of our contemporary innocents. For instance, it is believed that when King Henry VIII was expropriating the wealth of England's churches, he needed an excuse for closing the monastery of Glastonbury. There was a young man named John Horner, an orphan who had been raised by the old abbot. He informed the King's agents that the abbot had lied in reporting the total wealth of the abbey. The abbot was dragged by wild horses, then hanged and quartered. John Horner, chief witness for the Crown, was rewarded by being given one of the deeds to the church property, which, according to custom, was placed inside a piecrust:

Little Jack Horner sat in a corner,
Eating his Christmas pie;
He stuck in his thumb and pulled out a plum,
And said, "Oh, what a good boy am I."

Even the simplest rhymes are believed to have meanings hidden from the little gamesters. Take the unassuming counting-out game:

Haly maley tippery two,
Hocus pocus dominocus,
Out goes Y-O-U.

Authorities aver that "Haly maley" is the "Hail, Mary"
of the Church, that "Dominocus" refers to the sacred
"Domine," and that "Hocus pocus," shared with magi-
cians for hundreds of years, derives from the ritual of
the mass with its impressive, "Hoc est corpus."

This sort of conjecture can be great fun, and is recommended for people who like double-acrostics and
word games, but it has led to remarkable excesses of
deduction. One analysis of Mother Goose proved that
Queen Elizabeth was the cat in "Hey, Diddle Diddle,"
the lady who rode to Banbury Cross, and "Mother
Hubbard," reigning without a consort. In 1834, Ker
proved to his personal satisfaction that "Ding Dong
Dell" was an anti-Church pasquinade, imported from
Holland. In 1842, Halliwell decided that "Lucy Lock-
ett" was based on the life of a famous courtesan, and in
1930, Katherine Elwes Thomas observed that "Bo-Peep"
was, without doubt, Mary, Queen of Scots.

Some of these speculations might very well be ac-
curate, but they are as valuable as the surmise that
Hamlet was not written by Shakespeare, but by another
man with the same name. But it is pertinent to our
purposes to point out that nursery rhymes have been
used for social satire and shall probably continue to be
of service in the political arena. We have seen many
cartoons depicting some foreign government or business enterprise as an egg cracked into a thousand frag-

ments. We know, without looking at the caption, that "All the King's horses and all the King's men" can't restore that government or set that business back on its feet.

And we all recognized the allusion when the lampoon appeared showing the Washington influence-peddler enjoying a large pie labeled "$10,000 Lawyer's Fee," while the caption noted, "Oh, What a Good Boy Am I." A recent candidate for high office found his way blocked, in part, by religious considerations. The cartoonist showed him considering a large votive candle planted firmly in the middle of the road leading to the official post. Naturally, the caption read, "Jack, Be Nimble."

As we have pointed out earlier in this chapter, songs written especially for children were not in abundance in early England. But the need must have been tremendous because the few new songs were sung and spread around with a speed that was astonishing. An example of a song written especially for small voices is "The Marriage of the Frog and the Mouse." It was first reported in 1549, as an example of our "sueit melodius sangis." By 1611 it was printed as:

It was the frogge in the well,
Humble-dum, humble-dum,
And the merrie mouse in the mill,
Tweedle, tweedle twino.

The story remained constant, but the chorus underwent drastic surgery. By 1705, it was published as:

"Heigh ho!" says Brittle,
With a namby, pamby, mannikin, pannikin,
"Heigh," says Barnaby Brittle!

When I was a boy in Canada, I learned an even more intricate version:

Cai madeiro, down to Cairo,
Cai madeiro, Cairo,
Straddle addle addle, bobble addle, bobble inktum,
Rinktum body minchicambo.

This may have been a distortion of the already distorted pseudo-Latin chorus:

Rigdum bonum duo coino,
Coi min ero giltee caro, coi min ero coino,
Stim stam pammediddle lara bona ringcan,
Ringcan bonum duo coino.

The song is to be heard in most children's schools, and is enjoyed in many of our best nurseries. It has been published as a prize-winning book by John Langstaff, illustrated by Maurice Sendak. It has been recorded a hundred times, just recently as a popular song. It has been made into at least three motion picture shorts, including a lovely puppet production by Louis Bunin. I mention all these vital statistics to show what can be done in our modern world with a simple story song written hundreds of years ago to amuse the children.

Children, however, do not themselves require special "children's songs." Many favorites of the world of childhood cannot be sung in public even for an adult audience. I would be severely censured if I should perform "Sweet Violets," "The Darby Ram," and "Lulu Had a Baby" for the children who first taught me the words. Yet, parents have told me that their tiny offspring love the ribald songs I've recorded. Although the language is a little above their low-slung heads, the children enjoy the rhythm and the spirit of ribaldry. In fact, any song can be a "children's song."

In performing for children in thousands of concerts in many cities, I have used ballads and songs which aren't considered juvenile fare. But even the dullest song can be enjoyable if a trick or a game is appended. At one performance, I was asked by an adult observer to sing, "Drill, Ye Tarriers." With some misgivings I began the song, wondering whether I could keep the attention of the toddlers for long. To my surprise, the three- and four-year-olds began waving their arms whenever I sang the word "Drill." I repeated the chorus a few times, and accentuated the key word. Soon we were playing an exciting game in which even the adults joined. It's easy to see how word games, such as "The Twelve Days of Christmas," can capture the audience, but we can go much further in finding grist for our song-mill.

Let's take that sophisticated adult production, "Greensleeves":

Greensleeves was all my joy,
Greensleeves was my delight,
Greensleeves my heart of gold,
All for my lady, Greensleeves.

Musically, it's a little difficult for beginners—not like "Loopety Loo," or "Walking Across the Green Grass." And although I've seen it sung to accompany an old English comic dance, the words aren't exactly filled with the essence of gaiety. But just tell the children that they are to raise their elbows on the word "Greensleeves" as if they were wearing sleeves of that color. It'll be great fun. You can do even more, if you can steel your heart to the job:

Alas, my love, you do me wrong
To cast me off discourteously,
For I have lovèd you so long,
Delighting in your company.

You can tell them to put their right palms to their foreheads on the word "alas." On "You do me wrong," they must point an accusing finger at the head in front of theirs. On the phrase, "to cast me off," they are to simulate throwing a bundle into the aisle. When they sing "For I," let them touch hand to breast sadly. This helps with the beat since it makes a wonderfully resounding "thwack." When they sing "you so long," the accusing finger is again indicated. And "delighting in your company" deserves a joyful throwing up of hands to the accompaniment of a wide-mouthed phony smile.

The preceding exercise may forever sour the observing adults on "Greensleeves," but it will delight juvenile audiences. I really have never used "Greensleeves" in this fashion, but I have performed this reconstruction job on many other songs which at first glance would seem to be much less likely subjects for children's songs. There isn't a song in the songbag that can't be made into a "children's song," and there isn't a folk singer in the country that couldn't use some new material for his children's programs. "Jimmy Crack Corn" and "I've Been Working on the Railroad" can go only so far.

Today, the main forum for children's songs is in the camps and the schools. Camp songs are often subjected to the kind of treatment we gave "Greensleeves." The schools held out against folk music for a long time, but have lately climbed on the ballad wagon. School music books used to contain songs, such as "The Little Thrush in the Eucalyptus Tree" or "Santa's Deer Dance," composed by the Music Teacher or the local music-district supervisor. It is still often true that the local music-district supervisor writes the book for his local music district, but now the folk songs predominate. These are often obtained by the supervisor after intensive research through someone else's songbook collection.

Another flourishing industry dependent on children's songs is the record business. Back in the early forties, there wasn't much for the small listener apart from "Tubby the Tuba" and "Peter and the Wolf." Then parents began to buy recordings of play-party songs as performed by such artists as Gene Kelly and Bing Crosby. The folk song, as intoned by Danny Kaye, Mary Martin, or even Lionel Barrymore, was soon a great source of income for record companies.

One day in the middle forties, a company called "Young People's Records" revolutionized the industry by putting out disks carefully chosen by qualified educators and psychologists. The company sold a phenomenal number of records and was then swallowed up by The Children's Record Guild, a new firm established by YPR's former president. The large record companies tried to emulate the style and quality of the two pioneers, and many even released some commendable disks. In fact, The Little Golden Records were of remarkably high caliber. But soon the parents stopped buying the 78's, and The Children's Record Guild languished. Then the other companies reverted to their old habits and again began releasing old and new songs promoted largely through the prestige of famous or notorious personalities. This system still works, since, for the most part, children's records are not purchased by children, but by parents who love big-name artists.

Television has experimented with folk music, but with little success. Of course, very few children's shows of any quality have lasted, so the failure of folk songs shouldn't be surprising. In many of the shows currently telecast, however, folk music is often used, especially where audience participation is desired. And I have recently performed for WNBC-TV a historical series in which American folk music was the thematic material.

Finally, there is that wild greedy beast, the popular song hopper, which is constantly in need of sustenance. Many a children's song has become the song fare of the teen-age record buyer. In a few cases, this has been only proper, since many of the songs of childhood were once adult material. One example is "The Dolly with the Hole in her Stocking," formerly a minstrel song by Cool White, then a play-party song, "Buffalo Gals."

Remember the "Dilly Song"? Well, in 1948 it won the most-likely-to-be-sung award in America and England, almost three hundred years after its first printed version appeared. In the original, a bawdy little chantey, the young country man suggested to his young country lass that they "must lie together." And even in 1805, when children had already adopted it for their own, a version included in "Songs of the Nursery" ended with the suggestive words, "And you and I will keep the bed warm."

In 1943, "Mairzy Doats" was everybody's favorite, derived from some lines in an old game song. Today, children are singing new versions derived from the popular song rewrite of the early game-song. The same is being done with "A Tisket a Tasket," "Paper of Pins," and "Hush, Little Baby," all of which scaled the heights of popularity. It's likely that the song-pluggers will eventually work their way through *Mother Goose* from cover to cover, and then they'll still be able to exploit the new versions of the songs as sung by the contemporary children who have heard the rewritten pop-songs based on their own original material.

As years pass by, the child tends to forget his favorite nursery songs and turns to the more synthetic products peddled by modern mass media. Many experts claim that the old songs are completely forgotten, but we believe that they lie dormant on the periphery of the adult consciousness, waiting to work their way to the fore during moments of stress or of secret relaxation in the sanctuary of the shower. Of course, the adult can always try to exorcise the songs of childhood by teaching them to his own progeny. In fact, that's how it all began. And that's how it keeps going.

3.

Sources of American Song

Franklin Delano Roosevelt once wrote, "We in the United States are amazingly rich in the elements from which to weave a culture. We have the best of man's past on which to draw, brought to us from all parts of the world." Our folk music partakes in this foreign heritage. Our folk songs are the product of an imported citizenry, our ballads and stories are among our most glorious hand-me-downs.

Our first Americans, the Indians, contributed very little to our songbag. Cadman and MacDowell might have been inspired by the Indian melodies, but folk singers were not. In an obscure version of "The Wayfaring Stranger," there is a phrase which sounds like a

Pawnee deer dance melody, but this is probably a co-incidence. Indian rain dances are performed all over our country, but only by Indians, and usually in very dry seasons, or during rich concentrations of tourists.

Why did the early immigrants ignore the Indian music? B. A. Botkin, in his *Treasury of Western Folklore*, cites the wry question that Scout Jim Bridger asked a frontier raiding party, "Well, boys, did yer kill 'em all or did yer leave some for seed?" And William R. McDaniel, in his *Grand Ole Opry*, suggests that "since the white man's attitude toward the Indians was generally hostile there was little fraternization and little intermarriage. Therefore, aboriginal music exerted little or no influence on what we now call American music." Parenthetically, we could add that the Indians' attitude toward the white man wasn't one of passionate admiration. Indian tribes which often guarded their music from other tribes would not readily perform for a white man's amusement.

But mutual hostility isn't the only answer. To European ears, the Indian music sounded ridiculous and unsingable. The Dutch, English, and French settlers scorned the aboriginal melodies as "savage." And the language barrier was tremendous. An Englishman might recognize a few words in a French or Spanish song, but "native" lyrics were a mass of repetitive gibberish. Had the Indian translated some of his songs into English, there is a slight possibility that these might have been learned by the frontiersman. This was never done. Consequently, our earliest folk music was imported.

Our earliest homespun songs, sung to imported

melodies, invited further immigrants to share the blessings of our continent. In 1802, "Jefferson and Liberty" predicted:

Here strangers from a thousand shores,
    Compelled by tyranny to roam,
Will find amid abundant stores
    A nobler and a happier home.

In 1848, another song, "Uncle Sam's Farm," repeated the message of welcome:

We have room for all creation,
    And our banner is unfurled
With a general invitation
    To the people of the world.
Come along, come along, come when you can,
Come from ev'ry nation, come from ev'ry land.

Many of our early songs were invitations to foreign unfortunates. The response of the recipients brought to our shores hundreds of Old World songs.

Despite these open-handed invitations, each immigrant group was greeted with hostility by the settled population. If mutual enmity were enough to prevent the acquisition of new songs, ours would be a poor culture indeed. The Dutch hated the come-lately English, the English despised the Germans, the Germans sneered at the Irish, the Irish lamented the coming of the Jews, and today's Spanish-speaking newcomers are being accorded a similar welcome.

As each new wave arrived upon our shores, the settled "Americans" enriched our folklore with songs and

stories describing the invasion of "cheap competi-
tion," "unwashed un-Americans," "foreign speech patterns," and "rowdy children." And the earlier settler
rarely failed to comment on the frightful way whole
families crowded into one room. Conestoga wagoners
in Pennsylvania made up verses to lament the arrival
of Irish immigrants on our shores:

The ships they will be coming here
　With Irishmen in loads,
All with their picks and shovels
　For to work on the railroads.
And when they come upon us,
　It is then we will be fixed,
For they'll fight just like the devil
　With their cudgels and their bricks.

　　In the early days, the language barrier, the hostility
of first-generation Americans, and the desire "to keep
the old bunch together," kept the newcomers in cultural
ghettos. Even today, the mining settlements in Illinois,
Kentucky, and Pennsylvania are rich in Welsh music
—for the mines were salted with men from Rhondda,
Llanfyllin, and Aberystwyth. In Minnesota and Wis-
consin, Scandinavians celebrate their national holidays
in colorful old costumes and dance and sing the traditional songs of their forebears. In the Pennsylvania
German country, one can still hear a song sung by the
Palatinate immigrants aboard their leaky America-
bound ship:

We fear no peril on the sea,
For God is watching everywhere.

We trust in Him to speed us on
To Christmas in America.

Cantonese folk songs flourish among our Chinese-speaking citizens. It is even possible to find among the singsong accents a few staid phrases of Mandarin. There are many fine Flower Drum Songs extant in New York City and San Francisco. These were created by the harassed population of Feng Yang, a province so devastated by floods, droughts, hurricanes, and plagues that each year the inhabitants were forced to take to the road as beggars. They would beat their flower-ornamented drums and sing:

Sing Feng Yang, play Feng Yang,
Feng Yang was a miserable land,
That was wasted by the flood,
Drought and storm from the mountains of the north,
Rich men took to lowly trade,
Poor men sold their sons out of hand.
I have no more children to sell,
With my flower drum I beg around.

There are many such Chinese songs in our land. But these are not the songs we refer to when we speak of traditional American song, or American folk song. Polish communities sing many Polish songs on Pulaski Day and on other days of the year. Some of their polka orchestras have even attained national popularity. Our Spanish-speaking immigrants brought with them a music which was greeted with great pleasure. Nevertheless, foreign-language songs are not the basic material of American folk music.

There is a special category which should be noted at

this point. Once in a while, a foreign song is translated into English and ingratiates itself into our songbag. Welsh singers for centuries knew "All through the Night" as "Ar Hyd Y Nos." "We Gather Together" was a Netherlands song long before it became our national Thanksgiving hymn. "Malbrouck S'en Va-t-en Guerre" is now "He's a Jolly Good Fellow." And everyone knows "Santa Lucia."

There is another group of songs which is even more insidious—the secret import. For years I have sung a wagoner's song, believing that it was one of our few indigenous products:

I have gone down with my wagon
Loaded up with pretty maidens,
By the time I reached the market
They were laughing and singing.
Well, long as I live I'll always drag on
Any pretty maidens in my wagon.
Whoa, Dobbin, whoa.

A year or two ago I performed the song at a concert and it was proved to me by a member of the audience that the entire product was a translation of a German favorite. The pretty maidens had once been "schoene Maedchen," and the final line, the exhortation to the horse, had originally been "Halte, Schimmel, halte." There are a few other such songs, but, once again, I would conclude that the foreign-language song has had little influence on the major body of American folk music.

Our national language is the key to our national song.

We speak a corruption of Shakespeare's English. For that reason, the British influence predominates in our folk song heritage. Our earliest songs were well known to the Bard of Avon, who was a highly esteemed tavern singer in his own right. Our earliest colonists were steeped in the traditions of Elizabethan England, and, in Elizabethan England, everyone was a musicmaker. The farmers and yeomen sang lusty ballads, the shepherds sang of their tedious duties, and the court poets sang of the idyllic life of the shepherd. The tiny isles were brimming over with folk song, and generous helpings were exported to the colonies.

The exportations from England took the form of remembered songs and of broadsides printed in London for the American trade. These broadsides included many old ballads and some new songs written especially about hangings, sinkings, and murders. They were sold to the colonials for a penny a sheet. Enterprising colonials went into the ballad-making business themselves. One, Benjamin Franklin, tells in his *Autobiography* of writing two broadside ballads, "One was called the 'Lighthouse Tragedy' . . . and the other was a sailor's song, on the taking of Teach (or Blackbeard), the pirate." According to Franklin, the first sold wonderfully because it was very timely.

Another English source of American folk music was the Psalm Books. In "The Courtship of Miles Standish," Longfellow describes Priscilla:

Open wide on her lap lay the well-worn psalm-book of
    Ainsworth,
Printed in Amsterdam, the words and the music together,

Rough-hewn, angular notes, like stones in the wall of a
    churchyard,
Darkened and overhung by the running vine of the verses.

The Ainsworth Psalter was a book of psalm translations set to simple tunes by Henry Ainsworth, one of
the Separatists on the Mayflower. Ainsworth felt that
it was important to write new tunes because the ancient
Hebrew music, "God's music," had been long forgotten.

In 1640, in Cambridge, Massachusetts, America's first
book was published. This was a collection of religious
lyrics called *The Whole Booke of Psalms*, known generally as *The Bay Psalmbook*. With this book, a preceptor
would "line out" a line from the book and the congre-
gation would repeat the line, chanting out pages at a
time. Psalmbooks were very popular, and in 1721 the
Reverend Thomas Walter even wrote an instruction
book for singing these songs. The book was printed by
Ben Franklin's older brother, who had commissioned
Ben to write the broadsides mentioned above.

Franklin, like many others, realized that songs about
contemporary events sold better than old ballads. However, in the absence of creative minstrels, most of the
earliest were set to the tune of some fairly well-known
melody. And so, besides the thousands of songs, from
simple lullabies to bawdy tavern glees, imported whole
from England, thousands of variations appeared. At
first there were only minor changes. Samuel Pepys, who
reported the singing of "Barbara Allen" in his *Diary*,
would have been surprised to hear this American version:

In New York Town where I was born,
And where I got my learning,
Poor Major Andre fell in love
With lovely Peggy Arnold.

Another use of "Barbara Allen" by colonists was for the long "Ballad of Sergeant Champe":

Come, sheathe your swords, my gallant boys,
    And listen to the story,
How Sergeant Champe, one gloomy night,
    Set off to catch the Tory.

In this case, "the Tory" was Benedict Arnold, and Champe was unsuccessful in his daring exploit. The song, however, was very successful and was one of many parodies on the ballads inherited from England. In 1754, an officer of the Maryland Independence Company composed a song to the melody of the English "Over the Hills and Far Away":

Over the rocks and over the steep,
Over the waters, wide and deep,
We'll drive the French without delay,
Over the hills and far away.

More and more English songs were stripped of their lyrics so that new words could be written for the music. By the time of the Revolution, the Continental Army was singing a thousand anti-British songs to English melodies. For example, William Boyce in 1759 composed a sprightly march in honor of the British Navy. David Garrick wrote the lyrics:

Come cheer up, my lads, 'tis to glory we steer,
To add something new to this wonderful year,
To honour we call you, not press you like slaves,
For who are so free as the sons of the waves.
Hearts of oak are our ships, jolly tars are our men.
  We always are ready,
    Steady, boys, steady,
We'll fight and will conquer again and again.

The rebellious colonists stripped the song of its lyrics
and created one of our first great revolutionary songs:

Come join hand in hands, brave Americans all,
And rouse your bold hearts at fair liberty's call,
No tyrannous acts shall suppress your just claim,
Nor stain with dishonor America's name.
In freedom we're born and in freedom we'll live,
  Our purses are ready,
    Steady, friends, steady,
Not as slaves but as free men our money we'll give.

The new lyrics were provided in 1768 by John Dickin-
son, among the first to turn the English-born songs
around to be aimed at the motherland. Throughout the
War for Independence, the luckless Redcoat was fired
on by English-trained militiamen singing parodies to
British songs.

And so our songbag grew, with such rewrites as:

What a court hath old England
  Of folly and sin,
Spite of good men like Chatham,
  Barre, Burke, Wilkes, and Glynn.
Not content with the Game Act,
  They tax fish and sea,

And America drench
  With hot water and tea.
Derry Down Down Down Derry Down.

The dynamic force of the English folk song has never expended itself. There are many songs still extant in America which are truer to the seventeenth-century versions than any in England today. There are thousands of English songs in America in which a word or a line has been altered, but little else. And there are thousands of songs created in the United States which seem wholly new, but are compounded of melodic phrases, verses, and old sentiments derived from the early ballads.

Just one recent example may help demonstrate this Anglicization factor in American music. A short while ago the most popular "pop" song in America was the story of "The Battle of New Orleans"—the story of a British defeat at the hands of Andrew Jackson. The words were written by balladeer Jimmy Driftwood (James Morris) of Arkansas, to the tune of the old fiddle tune, "The Eighth of January." According to all the newspaper and magazine accounts, this melody had been written in 1815 to celebrate the victory at New Orleans. But, in fact, the tune has been fiddled around the British Isles for centuries.

The "Eighth of January" is no exception. Our English folk song legacy is not just a pile of historical documents covered with undisturbed cobwebs. Our continent is crammed full of British-born folk music, which is the single most important generating factor in our American music.

The next great influence on American song was that
of the Irish bards. Fleeing from poverty, debt, starva-
tion, and humility, the Gael brought with him a music
so vital and compelling, sung often in the prevalent
English tongue, that it made an immediate impression
on our unfriendly early settlers. They loved the songs
and hated the singers:

I'm a dacent lad just landed from the town of Ballyfad;
I want a situation and I need it mighty bad.
I heard employment advertised;
   "Tis just the thing," say I,
But the notice ended with the words,
   "No Irish need apply."

The Irish immigrant provided musical accompaniment for American lyrics on countless subjects. In fact,
the "Wagoner's Song" with (p. 36), its anti-Irish refrain, was sung to "The Wearing of the Green." The
Irish gave us such vaudeville classics as "The Mulligan
Guard," "Mother Machree," and "The Garden Where
the Praties Grow." They also contributed the lovely
airs, "The Inniskilling Dragoon," and "She Moves
through the Fair." Many of our "indigenous" songs are
really altered Irish imports. For example, the traditional
cowboy song, "Get Along, Little Dogies," is sung to a
sad Irish lullaby:

As I was a-walking one evening for pleasure,
   Down by the still waters I joggled along,
I met an old man making sad lamentation,
   And nursing a baby that's none of his own.
"Ee-ay-oh, my laddie, lie easy,
   It's my misfortune and none of your own,

That she leaves me here weeping and rocking the cradle
  Minding a baby that's none of my own.

One more example should be enough to establish the impact of Irish music on American life. This is the tale of "Rosin the Beau," which is still sung in Ireland and in America as it was known to the first Irish immigrants:

I live for the good of my nation,
  But my children are all bending low.
Still I hope that the next generation,
  Is more like old Rosin the Beau.

Irish immigrants sang it in the New World until the melody was one of the best-known in the land. It became a popular fiddle tune with the appropriate title, "Rosin the Bow." When Henry Clay was called upon to run for the Presidency, his campaign song was "Gallant Old Hal of the West," which bore the notation, "To be sung to the tune of 'Rosin the Beau.'" The Lincoln bandwagon rolled on to the same tune with the lyric:

Hurrah for the toast of our nation,
  Our hero so brave and so true.
We'll go for the great reformation,
  With Lincoln and Liberty, too.

When the forty-niners set out for California, they took with them such staples as salt, ham, flour, and "Rosin the Beau." When they met with disappointment, they rewrote the song, with the following consequences:

I've wandered all over this country,
  Prospecting and digging for gold;

I've tunneled, hydraulicked, and cradled,
   And I've been increasingly sold.
So throwing my grub on a blanket,
   And leaving my pick on the ground,
I started next morning to shank it,
   To the country they call Puget Sound.
No longer the slave of ambition,
   I jeer at the world and its shams;
I gaze on my happy condition,
   Surrounded by acres of clams.

"Acres of Clams," née "Rosin the Beau," once was the State Song of Washington, but the little air left its traces in all of our fifty states. Hillbilly bands today play the melody for one of the best-known classics of country music, "Down by the Willow Gardeen."

The success story of "Rosin the Beau" was one of many. Lumberjacks, railroaders, boatmen, dishwashers, and carpenters constructed their own special lyrics to "The Wearing of the Green," "The Girl I Left Behind Me," and "The Irish Washerwoman." Square-dancers promenaded to the tunes of "Soldier's Joy," and "Haste to the Wedding." "The Streets of Laredo" had once been sung as "The Bard of Armagh," and the bards of Cork, Tipperary, and Down had bestowed upon Americans a great legacy. The Gael had restrung the lute of the English minstrel, and our folk music was tinted green.

The Scot, too, was important in American folk music development. However, his contribution was somewhere between that of the Irish and the English. It isn't necessary in these pages to list names, titles, and melodies of Scottish origin. We will merely indicate our gratitude to the "Isles" and continue.

Much of our early music was "square," with the stolid insistence of a dance teacher instructing a left-footed student, "One, two, three, four; one, two, three, four." The Gael, it's true, jigged a bit. The Briton lilted once in a while. But nobody really jumped until the African arrived. Shanghaied into dank, filthy holds of slave ships, the immigrants from the Dark Continent made us a gift of the syncopations, polyrhythms, and blues notes which made our music the envy of the world. And, because the African learned to speak English, there was much traffic in song on the plantation of the South.

The spirited drummer boy of '76 often beat out a stirring tattoo, but the African could balance the ritual sound of fifty log-drums all beating in separate patterns. Consequently, while the white masters were chanting hymns in careful measures, their slaves would be shouting the same song and beating out stirring counter-rhythms on tambourines, gourds, and logs—foot-tapping and hand-clapping all the while. When the excitement spread, infusing the slave rhythms into the Protestant church liturgy, the country witnessed the frenzy of hysterical revival meetings and "shouting" Sunday meetings.

The African, furthermore, refused to be limited by our Western musical scale with its twelve notes. His musical background was richer and greatly creative. For instance, one of the representative instruments he had used was the "mbira." This usually provided ten notes, a few of which, it is true, sounded like those employed by Beethoven, Bach, or Brahms. However, the arrangement of these notes would startle even a pupil of Hindemith. The first note, obtained by bending and releasing a metal prong, might be middle C, plus or minus a few vibrations. The next might produce a dull "gunk." The next note might be another "gunk" or even the same middle C. Each tribe would make up its songs using its own version of the "mbira."

When two tribes met to dance and sing together, it was necessary that they agree on a mutual "mbira" for the joint musical endeavor. Many of the notes upon which they might agree would be unobtainable from our piano keyboard. These shaded notes we call "blues notes," and they can be found in the cracks between the piano keys. A "blues" singer learns to hang around the notes without resting too decisively on the exact musical value indicated on the staff paper.

Another import from Africa was syncopation, the insinuation of an accented beat where none is expected, the little hesitation which withholds a note for one tantalizing beat. Jazz was one of the results of the African influx. Gershwin, Gould, and Bernstein found inspiration in the African blues notes, the polyrhythms, and the syncopations. And the simple British-trained balladeer was also emboldened to extend his methods of performing.

For years the British tradition had tutored Americans in a tight-throated solo presentation of the old songs. But the African slave had been brought up in a musical atmosphere of choral singing, with easily produced

free tones sung in an animated manner. The slave singers, in other words, liberated our Anglo-shackled music,
and provided us with spirituals, work-hollers, patting
games, cakewalks, and a foot-tapping foundation for
our popular song.

American folk music, then, owes its existence to immigrants from every country in the world. But it was
the Briton and the African who, above all, fashioned
our national songbag, and gave the rest of the world
one more reason for envying the American people.

4.

The Antique Art

Why should an antique musical form be one of our most popular contemporary experiences? Usually the success of folk music is attributed by authorities to its time-tested qualities. It is presumed that a song that has withstood the erosion of the ages and the vagaries of human predilection has some considerable merit. In *The Ballad Tree*, Evelyn Kendrick Wells offers this comment: "The principal reason for the return of the folk song is the vitality that lies in the song itself. Because it was good, it has lived."

This Darwinian approach is not entirely satisfactory. Many taboos, superstitions, and unpleasant customs persist without any visible merit. Many of our most successful "folk songs" and folk-type songs, such as "Scarlet Ribbons," "The Battle of New Orleans," and "Sixteen Tons," are of recent invention. Time-testing alone is not the answer.

Ray M. Lawless, in his excellent survey, *Folk Singers and Folk Songs in America,* suggests that two world wars helped familiarize urban Americans with folk music. Certainly, familiarity with the sound of any musical form helps ensure its acceptance. Many a middle-aged folk music enthusiast traces his enthusiasm to some guitar-strumming "hillbilly" with whom he shared the war. Any survey of barracks ballads would certainly reveal that "The Wabash Cannonball" had the inside track. However, this wouldn't account for the multitude of peace-engendered teen-age fans. An explanation that doesn't account for that particular multitude must be considered incomplete.

Alan Lomax is one of the most astute observers of the American scene. In his *Folk Songs of North America,* he gives an explanation for folk music's popularity which seems to include "familiarity" and "nationalism." Says Mr. Lomax; "Folk song calls the native back to his roots and prepares him emotionally to dance, worship, work, fight, or make love in ways normal to his place."

Many readers will object to "familiarity" as not being applicable to America's urban centers—"few people were conversant with folk music in the past," it is argued. Actually, all Americans were once folk singers. As children they all sang "London Bridge," "Loopety Loo," "Skip to My Lou," and even such naughty an-

cients as "The Shades of Night." Adults, too, urban or
otherwise, know "The Man on the Flying Trapeze,"
"The Rambling Wretch," and "Abdul the Bulbul
Ameer." Collegians know volumes of well-worn bawdy
songs, and Rotarians meet weekly to sing "Old Man
Noah." And aren't we all Christmas audiences for the
carols chimed at us in department stores, railroad stations, and banks?

That the sound of folk music is not really unfamiliar
to the populace is a fact which has not gone unnoticed.
I have been asked by many publishers of great worth to
provide them with popular songs based on folk material. One of the most articulate invited me to "give us
some songs that everybody thinks he's heard before."
The appeal of the familiar is greater in that it is cumulative. The audience hears the familiar-sounding material; it asks for more of the familiar-sounding material;
the material becomes more familiar. After a season of
Belafonte, Kingston Trio, and Brothers Four records,
the audience is even readier for Belafonte, Kingston
Trio, and Brothers Four records. There are certainly
good reasons to credit the "familiarity" hypothesis with
the rebirth of the folk music vogue. However, I think it
is only a part of the answer.

Mr. Lomax seemed also to point to "nationalism" as
an important factor. This seems like a fruitful explanation. Our way of life is not only under attack, but has
sustained some exceptional reverses. We have turned
to each other, as if in surprise, for some communal com-
fort. These are times in which some of us have started
listening to our own voices singing the previously un-

noticed words of our national anthem. Perhaps "nationalism" is the answer.

Consider, in favor of this last, the fact that folk song and "nationalism" have gone hand in hand through history. The Revolutionary American had hundreds of songs before he adopted "Yankee Doodle." The contemporary "Scottish Republican Army" songsters contain as many good songs as did the Jacobite folios of Bonny Prince Charlie's Day. The I.R.A. sang so many songs we wonder that they had time to fight. The Nazis marched and fought to old German army songs and hundreds of Goebbels-inspired parodies. In Israel, there are music schools that graduate each year hundreds of composers with degrees in producing "folk music."

Furthermore, folk music is a very important element in the cultural armory of all fanatical nationalistic movements—in Africa, Asia, and South America. Most totalitarian countries accept as a maxim, "Art is one of our most important weapons." Consequently, they encourage their young people to rewrite the national songs to conform with the immediate policies of their leadership. Since "the line" is subject to sudden change, there exists in these countries an industrious group which busies itself with correcting daily deviations in ancient songs.

However, America's supernationalists, such as the D.A.R. and the American Legion, depend upon well-known patriotic airs for their inspiration. And folk music fans rarely associate their songs with the flag. In fact, many men in authority equate folk music with un-Americanism.

"Folk music, like a beard or sandals, has come to represent a slight loosening of the inhibitions, a tentative step in the direction of the open road, the knapsack, the hostel." So writes Susan Montgomery in *Mademoiselle*, in an article called "Folk Furor." For many, folk music has become an antidote to the conformity induced by our mass culture. In a way, it is antiestablishment. Critics who wish to belabor our modern communications media, our advertising industry, our big business institutions, and other manifestations of the American Dream, favor this explanation.

Most authorities agree that the specter of "conformity," real or imagined, haunts the youth of today. Large corporations, seeking recruits from among college graduating classes, turn down "troublemakers" however high their scholarship ratings. "Controversial" individuals, even if they earned their title battling recognized evils, are not the darlings of our polite society. For many, folk music is a socially acceptable manifestation of rebellion.

Many of the songs that are popular today remind the singers of the day when every frontiersman was a nonconformist. The old ballads abound with troublemakers and angry young men. There are scores of antiauthority songs in which the poor but honest bandit triumphs over the malefactors of great wealth, and the landlord loses his rent money and often his daughter to the renter. Possibly, singing these songs gives the adolescent the same release as is enjoyed by the child that calls its doll "Daddy" and then gleefully tears off its arm. Very possibly nonconformity has a great deal to do with the folk song vogue.

A theory that parallels the last is the "exclusivity" hypothesis. Experts aver that many folk fans took up the art in order to be different from the average American. As more people became aficionados, the early adherents were forced to espouse more esoteric forms of folk music—turning from Burl Ives to Bascom Lamar Lunsford, from Lunsford to Pete Steele, and from Pete Steele to whichever backwoods minstrel was as yet undiscovered by the masses. That this group does not represent the majority, and consequently will not answer the question posed in this chapter, is self-evident.

In contrast to the "exclusivity" theory we turn to an explanation of the popularity of "skiffle" in England. Skiffle is folk song with a jazz beat. In other words, it is the kind of music which has infiltrated American popular song. England's Lonnie Donegan with his Leadbelly-inspired "Rock Island Line" is the great exponent of the art. Brian Bird, a clergyman who is one of England's best-known musicologists, writes, "This need which skiffle is supplying—this need for friendship and co-operative effort—was in the past met by the Church, which throughout the Middle Ages and up to comparatively modern times did provide for people the opportunities for assembling for singing and dancing and self-expression."

The current "Singalong" fad would seem to affirm Mr. Bird's observation. Oldtimers, remembering the bouncing ball of the early motion picture programs, wouldn't call this a new trend. But for young Americans it's wonderfully novel. Many of the spectators at the national folk festivals bring along their own instruments and spend the time between concerts in communal performance. Musical togetherness accounts, in some small measure, for folk song popularity.

"According to experts, the basic cause of the bull market in folk music is the do-it-yourself trend." Thus spoke *Time* magazine in an article titled "Folk Frenzy." Any theory which bears the Luce imprimatur deserves careful study. The sales of banjos have increased five hundred per cent in the past ten years, and the National Association of Music Merchants reports that "four and a half million youngsters know at least four chords on the guitar."

It is an accepted fact that Americans succumbed to the "do-it-yourself" craze of recent years, ordering all sorts of kits, from T.V. sets to Voodoo equipment. Some are busy building sailboats in their basements. Others are busy building basements. Method books in guitar and banjo instruction are being printed on twenty-four hour schedules. One leading New York City music store has on display twenty-two folios called *How to Play the Guitar* which promise quick results to anyone who wants to learn.

Folk music has a special attraction for the self-doer; it is almost antiperfectionist. Professor Robert J. Potter of the Department of Sociology at the University of Michigan was quoted by David Riesman on this facet of the folk fad, "Folk music by its very nature doesn't make perfectionist demands with respect to perform-

ance, but is in some ways even 'better' if it is not perfect—imperfection makes it more folksy." Brian Bird
of England, previously quoted, has this to say: "It is a
home-made, 'do-it-yourself' music, within the reach of
all of limited means and no more than average ability."

We would go further than Mr. Bird. We would say
that folk music was within the reach of those with *less*
than average ability. Our nation is peopled with unfortunates who were tagged as "listeners" by harried
kindergarten teachers, and, consequently, fear the
sound of their own voices raised in song. But sub-
merged in an audience singing "Wimoweh," or skillfully
stamping the foot to the beat of "The Boll Weevil,"
they are finally able to express themselves.

Yet there is a flaw in the "do-it-yourself" position. I
have heard many comments from folk singing fans
throughout the country that concerts are being "over-
singalonged." I asked Peter Seeger, who has been
credited with responsibility for the revival, whether he
hadn't heard similar complaints. He agreed that there
had been some discussion of this problem, and that he
had started to cut down the audience participation por-
tions of his programs. Many folk song enthusiasts will
not sing along and will not play along. And a majority
of pop music fans would rather listen to a popular recording of a folk song than participate in its presentation. So, possibly, "do-it-yourself" is only a part of the
answer we've been seeking.

In a recent issue of a national magazine, Joan Baez,
whose folk song records have sold over 100,000 copies,
described her success in the coffee houses of Harvard

Square, "I sang to troubled intellectuals with the Bomb on their minds." Many authorities believe that young people have turned to folk music as an antidote to the insecurity of modern existence. Our contemporary world carries on its daily business under the sign and sword of Damocles. Issues which seemed very simple in the good old days are now viewed with dispassionate indecision. No longer do the heroes wear white hats and the villains wear black hats.

Young people looking for positive values can find them in the cowboy dramas or in the old songs. On campus after campus I have heard the lamentation that there have been no "great causes" since the Spanish Civil War. Nan Robertson, reporting in *The New York Times* concerning the new college "era of protest," points out that in actuality "the vast majority of American students remains quiet, inactive, and uncommitted." Our young people miss the giant-size heroes of the past, the heroes who people the world of folk music. Modern audiences are happy with the frontier ballads which are simple, direct, and dramatic.

In the face of this plethora of explanations for the current popularity of the simple sound, it is a marvel that no one predicted it. It is also a marvel that few of the experts have come forward with a definitive explanation. In an attempt to fulfil this need, I decided to turn from the commentators to the commented upon. In concert after concert in state after state I solicited answers from my audience to the question, "Why do you enjoy folk music?" In broadcasts on television and radio I continued asking for personal revelations. The general response was a surprise.

Of course, I received many highly personal communications which were interesting but unproductive. A pretty young lady in Chicago informed me, "I got interested in folk music because I got interested in a folk singer." One correspondent wrote, "I'd sing anything so long as it annoyed my brother." However, in most of the letters one idea seemed to be the key. "I like folk music because it's more meaningful than most of the pop songs." "When you listen to the old songs they seem to have more meaning." "Ballads mean more than most songs."

It took me a while, but I was able to ascertain to my satisfaction the significance of the word "meaningful." When we defined "folk song," I said I would accept under that title any song which had the simple sound usually associated with traditional music. I referred to the patina which makes the listener believe that the song has had a long journey to the moment of its present performance. It made no difference if the song were recently invented as long as it had the textural quality of historical expression.

This special quality, this simple sound, makes the singer believe that he is one of a long line of balladeers, and it enables the listener to persuade himself that he is hearing an expression of the drama of life long past. Each feels that he has been given an insight into the raw material of history. The young people of today, and many of the old people as well, find themselves one with the gnarled backwoodsman, and the cloth-shod Continental of Washington's time.

This may not be the definitive answer to the question we posed at the beginning of this discussion, but it's a very useful one. For instance, we can understand the nationalist now. He feels the songs are intrinsically American even when a lyric seems to inveigh against respectable national institutions:

The candidate's a dodger, a well-known dodger
The candidate's a dodger and I'm a dodger, too;
He'll call you friend and ask you for the vote,
Look out, boys, he's out to steal your note.

The nationalist smiles tolerantly, noting that Davy Crockett and his Alamo buddies probably did a little griping, too. Yet he knows *they* were 100% Americans.

The insecure generation feels a stabilizing identification with the ancients who presumably invented and perpetuated the songs. There have always been troubled people living through troubled times and a phrase or two in the repertory of the simple folk can always be interpreted in contemporary terms.

The nonconformist, too, has a field day with the songs. His rebellion has been mirrored in a thousand verses. When he listens to the old songs, he knows that *he* is the conformist, and that the smug and solid citizens who bedevil him are not only "square," but, according to the morality of the folk song, are "un-American" as well.

For the majority of the pop song enthusiasts, the folk song is a relief from the banalities of most popular lyrics.

Most of the old songs seem to be written in speech patterns that ring true to normal conversation. The rock 'n' roll fans are willing to accept unpoetic, often badly rhymed verse, in preference to the deliberate poesy attempted by Tin Pan Alley poetasters. "Truth" has touched them. Verisimilitude makes them believe in the communal reality of folk music.

For a while at least a song which has that "well-handled" feeling, which sounds like it has been sung by "those who have gone before," will enjoy great acceptance in America. In my opinion, it is the "simple noise" associated with traditional song which is the major reason for the current popularity of folk music.

5.

Setting the Stage

Today, folk music is a major industry. To revive it to this advanced status, it first had to become popular on a small scale in the centers of mass communication—New York, Chicago, and Los Angeles. This achievement was the result of the unorganized efforts of many individuals, groups, and political movements. Many of the movers and doers had other plans for the material.

We should really not be speaking of a revival at all. Folk music has never been close to extinction, even though early collectors believed that their sources were "the last surviving members," and that their printed versions were the terminal expirations of a dying art. In

1898, when the American Folk Song Society was established, the members dedicated themselves to the mission of gathering up the last remnants of folk music still surviving in America. It was believed that American folklore would soon be gone with the dodo, the auk, and the bison.

However, this has always been a singing country, stimulated by constant injections of new songs and new ideas accompanying the immigrants from the Old World. There has always been singing around such disparate areas as work camps, play streets, barracks, and campuses. There have always been such stirring singers as the Hutchinson Family of the 1860's, singing songs of protest and social commentary. The experts ignored all this material and concentrated on the remnants of ancient British ballads in America. And these were carefully guarded lest they be lost and American folk song be lost with them. This was the hothouse atmosphere of American folklore scholarship before John Lomax.

In 1895, this pioneer without portfolio set out for the University of Texas. In place of a portfolio, he carried among his effects a collection of cowboy songs jotted down on scrap paper, old envelopes, and pieces of cardboard. One day Lomax timidly showed some of the material to Dr. Morgan Callaway, Jr., author of "The Absolute Participle in Anglo-Saxon," "The Appositive Participle in Anglo-Saxon," and "The Infinitive in Anglo-Saxon." Callaway examined the rag bag of scraps courteously, though gingerly, and then informed Lomax that the frontier literature was tawdry, cheap, and unworthy.

Lomax thereupon folded his material, placed it back in his luggage, and continued his studies.

In 1906, Lomax enrolled in an American Literature course at Harvard, superintended by Barrett Wendell. For some fortunate reason, the tattered music papers were carried along on the trip to the Northeast. They might have stayed in the carpet bag had not Wendell assigned the class, on one occasion, to bring in representative selections from the literature of their native regions. Lomax was ready with his cowboy songs, even though folk music had been recently characterized in a newspaper article as "vulgar frothings."

Barrett started reading through the "selections from the literature of their native regions." In a short while he was bored with Emerson, Holmes, and Hawthorne—all proper Bostonians. And then he came to Lomax' contribution. He was fascinated and excited. And he promised the young Texan an introduction to George Lyman Kittredge, one of America's best-known scholars. Kittredge was the dean of American Shakespearian scholars, and he was also one of the leading folklorists of the day. In 1904, with Helen Child Sargent, he had published a beautifully edited edition of Francis J. Child's *Ballad Collection*. In a way, he was the leader among the scholars who thought of folk singing as "an antique art." But Kittredge wasn't afraid to measure his predilections against new evidence. Obviously Lomax' collection disproved the accepted belief that folk music was moribund. Kittredge began to relish the anticipated shock that awaited his colleagues. His smile and his nod were all the encouragement Lomax needed. But Kittredge and Wendell did more than just smile and nod. They helped draft a circular to be sent to hundreds of newspapers requesting help and soliciting song contributions. Then they arranged for a series of fellowships which were to help support Lomax on his projected field trips.

Emboldened by the newspaper publicity and the high regard of the educators, Lomax returned to Texas to speak at various functions and ask for help. He soon discovered that, in his native state at least, he was a prophet with little honor. When he tried to interest a meeting of the Texas cattlemen in his work, he met with unqualified derision. One cattleman even went so far as to make a short speech:

"I been singin' them songs ever since I was a kid. Everybody knows them. Only a damn fool would spend his time tryin' to set 'em down." Next the speaker moved an immediate adjournment to a nearby bar. The motion was seconded and passed unanimously.

Lomax persisted. He dragged his massive Ediphone machine, with its impressive recording horn, from county to county. When he had gathered a goodly lot, he paused for a while to examine the catch and to prepare a book. Then he brought the manuscript to D. Appleton & Company. The editors laughed at the whole idea. Until that moment, ballads and songs had been treated as vulgar poetry. Here was a young Texan collecting words *and* music sung by living human beings and asking a reputable company to put them in a book. It was ridiculous. At Doubleday, Page & Company, Lomax was given a short reception and a quick refusal.

A few more rejections followed. Then, to Lomax' surprise, a pair of New Yorkers named Sturgis and Walton decided to publish 122 texts. With some hesitation, they even agreed to include the music for eighteen of the songs. Had they published more of the music, it would have been a blessing for American folklorists, because, unfortunately, many of the cylinders later crumbled into dust, and the melodies as sung to Lomax were lost forever.

The book was launched with an introduction by Barrett Wendell in which he pointed out that the author had the support of George Lyman Kittredge. But it was an unexpected letter, reproduced on the flyleaf, which really forced the attention of the critics. Theodore Roosevelt, attending a Frontier Day Celebration in Cheyenne, was approached by Lomax and taken by his earnestness. He read through the manuscript of the book and congratulated Lomax on the song about Jesse James. He liked that one especially because Frank James had been one of T.R.'s most faithful adherents in Missouri. He wrote a letter for inclusion in the book—a hard-fisted endorsement of the contents and the author.

Despite the respected sponsorship, the reviews of *Cowboy Songs and Other Frontier Ballads* were not all laudatory. The *Boston Transcript* reviewer called the book "cheap trash." Lomax signed for a series of lecture tours to defend his work in universities and colleges. Meanwhile, he continued his collecting, sometimes borrowing material from other collectors. He began to compare his collected versions with material in university libraries and often listed as authentic material his own rewrites or reorganizations of folk songs. Later scholars have denigrated his work because of these lapses. But we must remember that Lomax was neither a scholarly researcher nor a true folklorist. If he had been either, he might never have produced such a tremendous body of work.

In 1933 Lomax and his son, Alan, then 17 years old and a junior at college, set out to record songs in the back alleys and corduroy roads of the South. With a 350-pound recording machine built into the rear of a Ford automobile, they traveled to penitentiaries and farmhouses, and recorded field-workers in sun-boiled, steaming swamps. They acquired hundreds of new songs—and malarial fever. In 1933, The Macmillan Company published the result, *American Ballads and Folk Songs*. The manuscripts were deposited in the Library of Congress, there to become the nucleus of "The Archives of American Folk Song," of which first John, then Alan, was to be Curator.

John Lomax was the great pioneer. Folklorists say that he should have listed his sources more carefully. It is said that there is evidence that he borrowed some copyrighted songs from other collections without credit. But it was Lomax who introduced most of our experts to folk music—the living art. And it is doubtful whether we would have had our current "revival" without his work.

The work of Alan Lomax has also been of major importance. Working with his father, and collecting on his own, he has produced books, records, and magazine articles in remarkable numbers. Before World War II his scripts for radio's "Back Where I Come From" demonstrated the power of contemporary comment in song. He taught actor Burl Ives many of the songs that Ives performed, and tried to make the material he found more meaningful by relating the songs to the life of the singers and the history of the country.

During his stay in Europe in the 1950's, Alan Lomax upset the staid, musty folklorists on the continent and in England by bringing in live ballad singers. Like our early folklorists, the European experts had assumed that they were dealing with material which was a legacy from the dim past. Alan taught them to look for the songs among their contemporaries. When he returned to the United States, in 1959, he left behind him hundreds of collectors whose claim to authority was a minor association with the dynamic American—the true son of John A. Lomax.

There were others working in the early days to obtain the raw material for today's popular song parade. In 1914, Josephine McGill traveled through the Southern Appalachians to find *Folksongs of the Kentucky Mountains,* published in 1917. Loraine Wyman and Howard Brockway's *Lonesome Tunes* was published after a similar journey in 1916. But these excellent collections were overshadowed by the appearance in 1917 of Cecil Sharp's *English Folk Songs from the Southern Appalachians.* Sharp was England's leading folklorist, and his skill at extracting variants of old songs was phenomenal. In forty-six weeks of travel through the Southern Appalachian Mountains, he collected 1,612 tunes. From this collection he was able, in 1918, to publish *American-*

English Folk Songs, and, from 1919 to 1923, his *Folk Songs of English Origin Collected in the Southern Appalachians.* Today, music publishers and performers draw heavily on the material collected by Sharp and published in 1932 as edited by his assistant, Maud Karpeles. Sometimes, the borrowers even credit the source.

Sharp was disdainful of the sentimental songs of the nineteenth century. He ignored these in his published works, and discouraged the singers who wanted to perform them during his recording sessions. Consequently, urban readers of his books never knew that these banalities were being sung in rural areas. But with railroads tracking into formerly isolated communities and with mining towns growing up in the midst of farmland, city songs were affecting the simple music. There were even a few pianos in farm parlors on which one could play sheet-music presentations of high-powered songs "as introduced in Tony Pastor's" and other metropolitan nightspots.

The country people tried to adapt the new songs to their old intonations. And they began to sing their old songs to the new syncopations and sophisticated rhythms. Soon "hillbilly" or "country" music developed. Recording companies, such as Gennett, Columbia, Brunswick, Victor, and Okeh decided that there might possibly be an audience which would pay for recordings of the music. They began searching for artists who could help reproduce the newly synthesized music, and Vernon Dalhart, Buell Kazee, the Carter Family, and many others were brought to country-wide recognition. Among others, Uncle Dave Macon recorded 100 songs between 1923 and 1938, some of these on the old *Vocalion* label.

In part, the interest in the songs was inspired by the collectors who were following the path of Lomax. Not only were they bringing unknown back-road singers to the attention of the public, but they were bringing the public to the attention of the singers. Collectors have observed that the simplest singer, learning that outsiders are interested in his simple music, begins to figure out ways of translating the interest into capital. Many country singers left for the city because some casual collector awakened hopes for easy money. The coming of the radio inspired many others.

By 1925, "Grand Ole Opry" was beginning to broadcast regularly on WSU in Nashville, Tennessee, and Uncle Dave Macon was its first big singing star. In the early days, the emphasis was on instrumental music played by groups with such bizarre names as "The Possum Hunters," "The Gully Jumpers," "The Snapper Whippers," and "The Fruit Jar Drinkers." In 1926, Ralph Peer, head of the Okeh record company, decided that his "old-timey" music catalogue was large enough to have its own section. He decided to name the music "hillbilly," though he knew that such major performers of the day as Bradley Kincaid thought "hillbilly" was an insulting epithet. The name was generally accepted, however, except by Bradley Kincaid, and the category boomed in sales. Blues and other Southern-accent material performed by Negroes was pigeonholed under the heading "Race," and, in some catalogues, can still be found with that title.

The repertory of "Grand Ole Opry" which has been popular for these many years is peppered with genuine folk songs and much folk-type material. Today it is the wellspring for much of rock 'n' roll and country music. This is another reason for our speaking of the present-day "revival" with reservations.

John Jacob Niles wrote, "In the beginning, there were only a few of us—and I mean very, very few." But Richard Chase, expert tale spinner and song collector, points out that the folk song "does not flare into sudden 'popularity' and then die out." It's interesting that most of the early pioneers thought of themselves as soloists—solitary gleaners in almost desolate fields. Nevertheless, besides the scholars we mentioned earlier, there were countless others—Joanna Colcord with her exciting collections of sea chanteys, Frank Shay and his disreputable books of masculine diversions, Robert Winslow Gordon, whose column in *Adventure* magazine, "Old Songs that Men Have Sung," built up a list of two thousand contributors in the years 1923 to 1927, and George Korson, whose stirring, "Songs and Ballads of the Anthracite Miner" (1926), contained over 300 songs.

Niles didn't reckon with these men and women, or with others, like Colonel Shoemaker and his light-hearted *North Pennsylvania Minstrelsy* (1919), or with Charles Finger's sturdy *Frontier Ballads* (1927). In fact, the same year in which Niles' first publication, *Singing Soldiers*, appeared, Harcourt Brace announced to the public the mammoth, poetic *American Songbag* of Carl Sandburg, with 280 songs.

Sandburg, with his ebullient personality and his

sprawling collection, made a tremendous impression in literary circles and among the book-reading public. Like Niles, the forelocked poet-balladeer was able to perform his songs for widespread concert and lecture audiences. His flamboyant stage personality and his lyrical musical expression gave the songs the drama they lacked on the printed page. And his book was full of sharp comments on our society and its participants. Today it is still a best buy for readers of literature, concert artists, amateur pianists, party singers, and popular recording artists.

In 1929, John Jacob Niles published *Seven Kentucky Folk Songs*. He also gave to Schirmer's manuscripts containing his own compositions, "Black Is the Color of My True Love's Hair," "I Wonder as I Wander," and "Venezuela." The first, a haunting song in the Elizabethan manner, was based on a traditional Kentucky song-lyric. The second was an original melody with extra verses written by Niles. The third was a complete fabrication. Niles, an accomplished composer, later explained that he didn't care much for some of the old songs and had decided "to honor them with my skilled attention." Important concert artists began to include these "simple folk songs" in their programs. Many concertgoers decided that there was great merit in folk music as a result of their exposure to the products of Niles's genius. "By 1930," Niles said, "I was singing folk music concerts everywhere and was quite solvent. . . . I composed along the way . . . such titles as "Go 'Way from My Window," "If I Had a Ribbon Bow," "The Lass from The Low Country," and "Jesus, Jesus, Rest Your Head."

In the early years of the depression, the Federal government decided to experiment in the collecting of regional songs. During this period men like B. A. Botkin joined the rapidly growing ranks of folk song aficionados. Newspapers all over the land published excerpts from these regional song folios, and the contrast between these and the pale productions of Tin Pan Alley helped turn many to folk music. Another product of the depression years was the emergence of the CIO and the left-wing movement. Rank-and-file unionists and left-wing political workers started using militant folk songs, many created in beleaguered factories or during duty on angry picket lines.

Following the example of the IWW—the "Wobblies" —of earlier days, the Communists, Socialists, and other left-oriented groups began to insist on folk songs at their meetings, parties, rallies, and picket lines. With few exceptions, the balladeers who began their careers in the 1930's gave many of their performances under radical sponsorship. Today these performances remain on record to serve as reasons for blacklists and investigations.

In 1934, the Lomaxes arranged a press meeting in New York City for Huddie Ledbetter, "King of the Twelve-Stringed Guitar." "Leadbelly" had been pardoned while serving a term for murder in a Texas penitentiary after a conviction for "assault with intent to murder." With the help of the fast-growing army of folk song enthusiasts, and an adroitly fashioned musical plea to Governor Pat Neff composed by Leadbelly, Lomax arranged for another pardon. Members of the New York Press were fascinated by the prison record of the performer and they were charmed by his music. They could hardly understand the lyrics because of Leadbelly's thick plantation accent, but they were moved by the power and raw emotion of his performance.

Lomax took Leadbelly on the university circuit. For some of the audience, it was more fun than a bear-baiting, but just about as culturally valid. But many remembered that vital figure on the stage beating out the rhythms and pounding out the lyrics of "Goodnight, Irene," "The Rock Island Line," "The Muleskinner Blues," and "Silvy." When Leadbelly sang "Midnight Special" and "The Boll Weevil," they began to foot-tap to their own surprised delight. Perhaps he was rough and crude, and his guitar-playing was often careless and untutored, but Leadbelly was a man. And his music was full of a joyful singing that was rare among the choked-up megalopolitans.

In 1936 the Lomaxes wrote the story of Leadbelly, as he told it, into a book, *Negro Folk Songs as Sung by Leadbelly*. It was our first exposition of the life of a singer, complete with his songs. It has been used since its publication as basic source material for the great "revival." Besides the songs mentioned above, the book includes "Po' Howard," recorded by the Weavers, "Roberta," recorded by Harry Belafonte, and "Take a Whiff on Me," recorded by Lonnie Donegan as "Take a Drink on Me." In fact, Lonnie Donegan's "Rock Island Line" recording was an almost exact imitation of a Leadbelly recording, complete with a cockney-shaded Negro-guttural introduction.

Another progenitor of the folk music rage was Joshua White. At the age of seven, Josh began to learn the songs of the blind men he led through the streets of Southern cities. And although these highly competitive streetsingers tried to hide their instrumental tricks from the boy, he managed to learn his melting guitar technique. In 1929 a representative of The American Record Company (later Columbia Records) offered Josh's mother $100 if she'd let her boy travel to New York City and record some songs. Mrs. White agreed if her boy was not required to perform any but religious songs. And so Josh White began his recording career as "The Singing Christian." Everything was going smoothly when the young gospel singer ran out of spirituals. Forgetting his mother's insistence, he began to sing his street-learned blues, which were released "as sung by Pinewood Tom."

Langston Hughes has said, "Josh White sings easy." Josh had to sing easy. Since he first came North, he has recorded for Keynote, Columbia, Disc, Asch, Perfect, Paramount, Decca, Musicraft, Apollo, Stinson, London, Livingstone and Vogue, with reissues by Harmony, Blue Note, Banner, Brunswick, Melotone, Oriole, Mercury, Emarcy, Elektra, and Ampar. His music crossed the dividing line between "race," "pop," and "folk." His precise throbbing guitar notes gave a virtuoso touch to the music which delighted even serious concertgoers. Later, when his recording of "One Meat Ball" became a surprise smash hit, he played Pied Piper to thousands of new folk music fans.

The bandwagon was picking up speed, impelled by such fine performers as Richard Dyer-Bennet, steeped in the cultivated traditions of the minnesingers and minstrels. A trained countertenor with an artful lute, he attracted many who had considered folk music too "low down." Dyer-Bennet sang folk songs as if they were art songs. His "John Henry" is a delicate ballad with graceful guitar figures. It is a tribute to his taste and artistry that many audiences found Leadbelly's "John Henry" unacceptable after hearing Dyer-Bennet's paraphrase.

As the dust covered the plains of the Midwest, tenant farmers and marginal income workers took to the road. They carried with them their rural songs as well as the "hillybilly" repertory. Among the wanderers was Woodrow Wilson Guthrie from Okemah, Okfuskee County, Oklahoma. Woody traveled and sang for money, making up new songs on the way. Louis Adamic wrote about him, "His songs are made out of what he sees and knows and feels; they are the living folk songs of America." Among the living folk songs that Woody made were "This Land Is Your Land," "So Long, It's Been Good to Know You," and a large number of militant labor songs about which he said, "They're especially good for workingmen who are tired of steady employment."

While Woody was making up songs around the country, new collections were appearing with increasing regularity. Ben Botkin put some of his Oklahoma folk material together for the delightful *American Play Party Song*, Helen Creighton produced *Songs and Ballads from Nova Scotia*, Mrs. Ralph Flanders (Helen Hartness) followed her collaboration with George Brown in

1932 on *Vermont Folk Songs and Ballads* with her 1934 *Green Mountain Song*. The rate of publication indicated a growing public interest in the simple music.

In 1936 an event took place which caused the left wing to swallow the folk music world almost whole. That year General Francisco Franco left Morocco with a small, highly disciplined force and assumed the leadership of the Rightist rebellion. The Loyalist cause seemed wonderfully pure and righteous. Even today one hears the plaintive regret that "Spain was the last great crusade." From all over the world volunteers sailed to join the International Brigade. English, German, Italian, and new Spanish words formed an alliance with the flaming flamenco melodies. These were exported to be sung at fund-raising rallies, and were recorded on stirring disks.

At every political meeting, at every street-corner rally, the Spanish Civil War songs were heard alongside the American product. Thousands of people who despised Franco and his allies, Hitler and Mussolini, learned about folk music as a result of that great campaign. Paul Robeson was one of the most popular singers of the day, presenting programs in which one could hear Sharp-collected songs such as "Oh, No, John," Spanish War songs, such as "Viva La Quince Brigada," and spirituals.

Young folk singers began to borrow liberally from the songbag created by the Grange Rebels in the days of William Jennings Bryan. City boys and girls began to learn to play guitars and mandolins in order to accompany the singing at parties and rallies. Soon these novices were sponsored by the Spanish Refugee Appeal, the

CIO, the Socialists, the American Youth for Democracy, and others. These groups, with their ideological emphasis on the welfare of the common man, found stimulation in the music associated with the common man. The left wing was so helpful in those days that many Americans believe to this day that folk music is a subversive art and that all folk singers are bomb-carrying Reds.

During this period, the Mightiest Balladeer of Them All was just managing to exist. Burl Icle Ivanhoe Ives had come to New York at the end of a wandering itinerary which began in Hunt City Township, Illinois. While he studied voice and acting in the City of New York, he sat in on folk song sessions with a motley group who called themselves "The Almanac Singers." The Almanacs kept singing, but Ives left his desultory employment as bus boy in International House to play in minor acting parts in unimportant shows. Then he graduated to a singing role in the musical, "The Boys From Syracuse." A few roles later, he began his CBS radio show, "The Wayfaring Stranger." This was one of the most important folk song programs in our narrative, and, along with Columbia's School of the Air series, it brought the folk song to a multitude of casual radio listeners for the first time. For the most part, Ives turned to Alan Lomax for his inspiration, and to John Lomax' collections for his material. But he also had some small songs of his own which made his program a daily delight.

Meanwhile, the Almanac Singers, without Ives, bummed around the country, singing for supper, lunch, and gasoline money. Joining the hard-core Almanacs— Lee Hays, Peter Seeger, Woody Guthrie, and Millard

Lampell—were singers such as Ives, Josh White, Bess Lomax, Butch Hawes, Earl Robinson, and Cisco Huston. Lampell is now a successful novelist, screen writer, and playwright (*The Wall, The Hero*, etc.). In later years, using his understanding of folk music and dramatic sensitivity, he wrote the stirring "Lonesome Train" with music by Earl Robinson.

Robinson differed from other singers of the thirties by being a trained composer. Like Niles, he had a degree in music and used folk song as raw material for serious compositions. His "Ballad for Americans" with a libretto by John LaTouche, his "The House I Live In" with lyrics by Lewis Allan, and his motion picture scores are redolent with traditional song. But his "Joe Hill" is one of our most stirring songs, and he still performs, with his own guitar accompaniment, the simple material which he may someday weave into an intricate symphonic pattern.

Cisco Huston was an itinerant actor and merchant mariner who was delighted with Woody Guthrie and his music. He took to the road with Woody and recorded with him some of the finest duets in folk song history. When Cisco died of cancer in 1961, he was on his way to popular success—having been rediscovered by a major record company. Before his death, he helped marshal the legions which would foster the rebirth of folk music along the Pacific shores.

From Little Rock, Arkansas, came Lee Hays, the powerful basso whose integrity and vocal chords carried a fair share of the Almanac harmonies. Lee was indebted to Alan Lomax for his espousal of folk music, although he had, as a young man, become acquainted with hymn singing. In his early recordings with the Almanacs, and in his later performances with The Weavers, his religious background shows up to advantage in the sonorous confluence of song.

Almanac Peter Seeger is still, as Chicago broadcaster Studs Terkel put it, "The tuning fork of America." In the days when he sang his left-wing-oriented songs with the Almanacs, Pete called himself "Pete Bowers" in order to avoid embarassing his relatively conservative family. His father, Charles Seeger, is one of America's most respected musicologists. Charles owes his interest in folk music to Thomas Hart Benton and the Lomaxes, and with his wife, Ruth Crawford Seeger, arranged the music for the Lomax collection, *Folk Song U.S.A.* When Pete was sixteen, his father took him to the Asheville Folk Festival in North Carolina. There Pete first saw the five-stringed banjo and, in his own words, "It was love at first sight." His travels through the country, alone and with the Almanacs, gave him one of the most extensive repertories of any of the folk singers in our history. And, without any major radio or television exposure—having been blacklisted for his left-wing activities—he has managed to become one of America's best-known and most influential balladeers.

The Almanac Singers performed wherever there was a sympathetic ear. With Peter taking many of the solos, they recorded the albums, "Talking Union," "Sod Buster Ballads," and "Deep Sea Shanties." They also recorded an album of antiwar songs, but when Russia was attacked by Nazi Germany this was withdrawn and another, "Dear Mr. President," was issued, urging full American participation in the war effort. Huston and Guthrie went off to sea with the Merchant Marine, Seeger went off to the South Pacific in an army uniform. The Almanac Singers were a casualty of World War II. But their records and performances touched the imaginations of enthusiastic knots of people throughout the country. They helped lead the way.

During the World War II, urban Americans in the Army and Navy were brought into contact with rural soldiers whose music filled the barracks after duty hours. Armed Forces Radio began presenting hillbilly songs and even some folk music. Radio was now the gold-plated entertainment medium, and a black-thatched writer-director named Norman Corwin was radio's golden-haired boy. Corwin believed that folk music had special dramatic qualities beyond the reach of popular music and he required his music composers to use folk themes in their scores. Besides this, he used Leadbelly, Josh White, Burl Ives, and Pete Seeger in some of his scripts, and in one case, he had the Almanacs in a final appearance singing Woody Guthrie's rewrite of "Old Joe Clark," retitled, "Round and Round Hitler's Grave."

I wish I had a bushel,
    I wish I had a peck,
I wish I had old Hitler
    With a rope around his neck.
Round and round Hitler's grave
Round and round we go,
Going to lay the poor boy down.
He won't get up no more.

Consequently, by the end of the war, Americans were not unfamiliar with the sound of folk music, and familiarity is part of the key to popularity. Another man whose work was of great importance in this area was Josef Marais. Marais was born in Lowry Pass, Union of South Africa. A trained musician, he was a concert violinist with a quick ear for learning many of the songs he heard during his concert tours of the Veld. During the war he worked for the BBC in London and used Afrikaans songs for their propaganda appeal. After the war he came to America and found that he could make a better than average living as a singer and guitarist. He was engaged to perform on "The African Trek" and "Koos The Hottentot," radio programs in which folk song and folklore were featured. Many of our most fervent folk fans trace their first contact with traditional music to the English translations of Afrikaans songs performed by Marais and his "Bushveld Band."

Another radio program which had some influence was WNYC's "Folk Song Festival." Although I had known Leadbelly, White, the Almanacs, and many of the others before the war, I had never tried to sing professionally the songs I had learned as a boy in Canada and in my travels throughout this country. But when I was discharged from the army in 1945, finding little work as a writer, I decided to offer my songs to every radio station broadcasting in New York City. I received a few invitations to perform and during the Christmas season I sang over WNYC, WNEW, WLIB, and WNBC. During this period Nathan Rudich, now publicity director for Otto Preminger, was Program Director of the Municipal

Radio Station. He and Herman Neuman, the Music Director, suggested that I stay on and act as "coordinator" of their folk music programs. At the time, Huddie Ledbetter was broadcasting for the station. Since Huddie was an old friend, my "coordinating" consisted mainly of walking down the hall on the twenty-fifth floor of the Municipal Building and waving to him during his broadcasts.

The practice at WNYC is to pay only the Civil Service staff, not the performers. Nevertheless, since 1945, every Sunday at 6 P.M. "The Folk Song Festival" has brought to the radio audience well-known personalities in the folk music world as well as hundreds of others with interesting material. As the years have flown past, visitors have begun appearing from all over our country. Of late, because of the rebroadcasts by the Armed Forces Radio Network and the United States Information Service, we have played host to singers from all over the world.

The WNYC show has been the only continuous folk song program in the country and, for that reason, has had a sizable influence. Children, grown up and living in other states, have used it as a model to present their own "Festivals" on local stations, and many folk-oriented pop singers were encouraged by public exposure on the "Festival" in the day when encouragement was needed.

In 1945, just when the WNYC show was inaugurated, Margot Mayo, whose American Square Dance Group was also promulgating the dance-song gospel, decided to have a "home-from-the-war" party. Leadbelly, Seeger, Dyer-Bennet, Niles, Guthrie, and many others performed. After the program, Peter Seeger came over to see me and asked if I would help him start a folk song magazine. We made immediate plans for a mimeographed publication, using the paraphernalia I had bought in Army days when I was editing a newspaper for psychiatric patients.

In order to get money to maintain the publication, which we named *People's Songs,* we decided to run a series of "hootenannies." This last was a word Pete had heard used by the Washington Commonwealth Federation to describe a folk singers jam session in Seattle in 1941. Among the performers was another important figure in the folk song movement—Tom Glazer. Tom had already achieved some fame singing in Washington with "The Priority Ramblers." His voice was one of the most mellifluous of all the singers' and his musical taste was impeccable. Soon he was hired to record children's records for the Children's Record Guild, Young People's Records, and many others. His songs, used in many schools, presented as Christmas gifts to thousands of impressionable children, were probably an important cause of adult fandom.

Musicologist Waldemar Hille, gentle and soft-spoken, became the musical arbiter of *People's Songs.* As each big hootenanny was held at Irving Plaza Ballroom, or the meeting hall of Local 65 near Astor Place in New York, Hille would convert the proceeds into a little magazine which sold few copies but was read by many. Labor and political songs were featured because the editorial board felt that students of other types of songs could find them in the now-abundant folk music collections.

As the magazine found its way to faraway places and college campuses, readers were excited by the outspoken lyrics and lively music of the "people's songs." The pervading atmosphere in those early postwar days was a "progressive" one which resembled the 1932-35 period. The worst was over, the future was filled with infinite possibilities, and the common man was to be once again enthroned. The unions, Communists, Socialists, and progressives began to hire folk singers again for every party, dance, and meeting. The left wing subsidized the folk singers to such an extent that one advertiser in the papers was impelled to note, "Rent party tonight. No balladeers will be present." By 1948, *People's Songs* had added a booking agency known as "People's Artists," and had helped arrange for many branches, including organized groups in San Francisco, Los Angeles, Chicago, and Boston.

There were hootenannies in colleges, among labor union educational groups, and at private parties throughout the nation. Folk singers' records were selling steadily. Folk songs were to be found in the music books being published for local boards of education. There were fans scattered all over the country—for "race," country, hillbilly, and folk music. The nation was ripe for the "revival." It was a new singing group, conceived at a hootenanny, animated by two veterans of the Almanacs, and inspired by the spirit of the Lomaxes, that ignited the spark. Before we further discuss this new group, it is important to take a look at the music industry they revolutionized.

6.

The Music Business

A popular song is not just an artifact, it is a mass-produced commodity. Today, few commodities are successful if they are not mass merchandised. Before we can talk about the success of folk music as a popular commodity, we should examine the mechanism by which popular songs are created and exploited. This mechanism is called "The Music Business."

We admit that there have been a few songs which have attained national popularity without the hard-sell packaging of the Music Business. Jack Paar's plugging of "Short Shorts," for instance, gave a semblance of life to a moribund bore. But, even then, Paar was using

the facilities of a mass-communications network to pro-
mote his spoof of pop music.

My next assumption will be disputed by thousands
of Americans whose nerves have been exacerbated by
twists, rock 'n' roll songs, and other public delights. It
is my belief that no amount of promotion will make a
"hit" out of a song which doesn't have a sound attractive
to the record-buying public. Many times popular
songs have been launched into the mart of public
opinion backed by bribes, publicity campaigns, and
giveaway offers. Many of these have failed miserably.

For example, it was believed for a while that a song
which did well in Detroit would capture a vast nation-
wide audience. One of my publishers, with great faith in
a folk song refurbished by me, set out for Detroit with
a fistful of dollars and a valiseful of influential intro-
ductions. A few weeks later my song was the big thing
in Detroit. And that's where it stayed. Short of bribing
each bobby-soxer and her male counterpart, there is no
way to force a song into the charmed "Top Ten." Nevertheless, there are many ways to insure that attention
will be paid some prospective winner.

It wasn't always thus with folk music. Take the song
"Chester," for instance. During the Revolutionary War,
William Billings wrote some melodies with tremendous
popular appeal. Billings, a Bostonian, was blind in one
eye, walked with a piteous limp, had a withered arm,
and, with his wife and nine children, lived in penury.
While Benjamin Franklin was enchanting his friends
with simple compositions on the guitar, Billings was
composing fuguing tunes. While Americans like Francis

Hopkinson, signer of the Declaration of Independence, were recomposing old songs, Billings was creating stirring orginal hymns. And his "Chester," even more than "Yankee Doodle," became America's first great anthem:

Let tyrants shake their iron rod,
   And Slav'ry clank her galling chains,
We fear them not, we trust in God,
   New England's God forever reigns.

Howe and Burgoyne and Clinton, too,
   With Prescott and Cornwallis join'd,
Together plot our overthrow,
   In one Infernal league combin'd.

Then there was the British drinking song dedicated to the bibulous Greek, Anacreon, who died, appropriately enough, choking on a grape seed. The song was the theme of the Anacreontic Society in London and was probably composed by Ralph Tomlinson. Many drinking societies in America knew it, and one of the most active—in drinking and in singing—was the Baltimore Chapter which had as its members many of America's most distinguished citizens. They sang the Anacreontic air until most of Baltimore knew the words:

To Anacreon in Heav'n where he sat in full glee,
   A few sons of Bacchus sent a petition,
That he their inspirer and patron would be;
   When this answer arrived from the jolly old Grecian—
      Voice, fiddle, and flute,
      No longer be mute;

I'll send you my name and inspire ye to boot;
And besides I'll instruct ye, like me to entwine
The Myrtle of Venus with Bacchus's vine.

The melody was a good one, but the words were a
little full-blown for simple people. Consequently, many
parodies were created and many new songs based on
the anthem. In "Adams and Liberty" one verse praised
America's first President to the tune of "Anacreon in
Heaven":

Should the tempest of war overshadow our land,
   Its bolts could not rend Freedom's temple asunder,
For unmoved at the portals would Washington stand,
   And repulse with his breast the assaults of the thunder,
     His sword from the sleep
     Of his scabbard would leap,
     And conduct with its point every flash to the deep,
And ne'er shall the sons of Columbia be slaves,
While the earth bears a plant or the sea rolls a wave.

During the War of 1812, one of the Baltimore society
members, a Dr. Beane, made the error of taking as
prisoners two British soldiers, an error since Dr. Beane
was a civilian, and besides, the area was under British
military occupation at the time. The foolhardy Doctor
was hustled aboard a British ship and threatened with
a possible death sentence. Another member of his
drinking fraternity, a lawyer named Francis Scott Key,
hurried to the British commandant and pleaded for
Beane's release. His eloquence was rewarded, and he
boarded the British ship to take his friend home. How-

ever, they were detained overnight while the British attempted to force the surrender of Fort McHenry with a tremendous bombardment.

Key wrote a song about his feelings during the engagement and, when he was put ashore, sang it for his friends. The song was put on broadsides and sold throughout the city to the tune of "Anacreon in Heaven," which everyone knew. The tiny nation was thrilled by the song and its fervor, and kept singing the song until, on March 3, 1931, President Hoover signed the bill making it our National Anthem.

Let's not underestimate the power of a song which could "sweep the nation" in our early days. True, the nation wasn't very big, but communications were slow. Any song which made the big time had to have something special about it. "Meet On Canaan's Shore" was small-time singing until it was rewritten to make "John Brown's Body." And even then it was comparatively insignificant until reissued as "The Battle Hymn of the Republic."

Some of our songs had the benefit of the fast-traveling minstrel circuit in their sweep to national fame. Stephen Foster's folk-type idylls were popular minstrel fare. So was Cool White's "Lubly Fan," which became "Buffalo Gals" in Buffalo, "New York Gals" in New York, and "The Dolly with the Hole in Her Stocking" all over the country. But no one tried to put these songs up for general sale. Folk songs traveled on their own steam or fell behind as the nation accelerated culturally.

By the time America changed over from an agricultural to an industrial society—in 1861—the songmongers were organizing their early sales machinery. Thousands of songs were written, published, and distributed among the civilians and soldiers. One commentator wrote, "It is worth fighting this war for the songs alone." But song-plugging was still a haphazard art.

It was John Philip Sousa who really showed the way. In 1892 Charles K. Harris was looking for a song to follow his "Kiss and Let's Make Up." An amateur minstrel group in Milwaukee asked him for a sentimental-type ballad. Harris wrote them a song about a headstrong youth who leaves his only love after discovering her kissing another man. Later he learns that the other man was her brother. "I broke her heart," he pines, "after the ball."

At the first performance of "After the Ball," the singer forgot the words. But Harris kept plugging it until it came to the attention of the great bandmaster Sousa who was then starring at the Chicago World's Fair. Sousa kept featuring the waltz tune until everyone knew it. It sold five million copies. Thousands of songwriters and publishers asked themselves the inevitable greedy question: "Why not me and mine?"

The new system seemed simple. Write a song, convince a popular artist to sing it, and collect the royalties thereafter. For instance, in 1896, Edward Marks and Joseph Stern were sitting in a German restaurant in New York City when a Lancashire waitress, pinched into anger, cried out that nobody would dare insult her if her brother Jack were present. The two publisher-writers

created "My Mother Was a Lady" on the spot, induced
Meyer Cohen to sing it the next night at Tony Pastor's,
and watched the sales climb.

For years popular songs were sold by way of the
"New York Performance" route, followed by sheet-music
sales to outlying areas. But in 1924, a phenomenon appeared which heralded a new era. A few years before,
Train Number 97, the fast mail train of the Southern
Railway had left the city of Lynchburg late on its way
through the Blue Ridge Mountains of Virginia. The
engineer, Joe Brodie, opened the throttle wide as the
train raced down the steep grade of White Oak Mountain near Danville. Unable to hold to the curving trestle
at the breakneck speed, the flier left the rails and
plunged into the ravine, killing most of its crew.

To the tune of Henry C. Work's, "The Ship That
Never Returned," balladeer David Graves George wrote
"The Wreck of the Old '97." In 1924, Victor Talking
Machine Company issued the record of Vernon Dalhart
singing the ballad. It sold more than a million copies.
Embarrassed, Victor advertised for the author, then unknown. Fifty writers advanced claims of authorship, including David George. In the ensuing litigation, none of
the claims was paid. But the hit recording and the publicity given the trials convinced the pop-music publishers that this was the twentieth-century way for achiev-
ing the "money song."

At the same time the fantastic little gadget known as
the crystal set was showing signs of maturity. At first the
consoles were gigantic. For instance, the Atwater Kent
radio was nicknamed "The Hot Water Can" because its

yard-square, five-foot-high body contained a condenser which required continual liquid replenishment. But it brought into the home such pioneers as "The Happiness Boys," Billy Jones and Ernie Hare, who laughed continually and sang popular songs. Other singers appeared on early programs, such as the Graybar Hour, and sang old songs and new ones with possibilities.

Folk music was ignored during this period on the major stations. But in Nashville, Uncle Dave Macon and Jimmie Rodgers led a host of entertainers whose broadcasts and recordings were important sellers in the South. In the North, Kate Smith and her mentor, Ted Collins, began looking for new material with which to create a feeling of variety. A singer could no longer be content with performing the same act all his life in town after town. The homogenized radio audience tuned in every week and expected a change of fare as a reward.

The song-plugger became an important middleman. These advertising men of the music industry began to stalk the managers, directors, and even the relatives of the radio stars. Sometimes they had lucrative deals for the artist who would sing the new song "specially created for you, baby." Performers such as Al Jolson began to receive a slice of the royalties for any song they helped put over. Recently, Abel Green, editor of the show business journal, *Variety*, was asked if this wasn't the forerunner of the modern blight, "payola." Green replied, "Jolson was contributing something he owned —his tremendous personality and showmanship—to the success of a song. But some of these A. and R. men, that's something again. That's like going to a restaurant for dinner and bribing a chef to make you a good meal."

An A. and R. man is responsible for the "artists and the repertoire" of a recording company. What Mr. Green is implying is that it is all right to pay a singer, but not a manufacturer. But more important is the recognition that years before the public was aware of it, the popular song was already being bought and sold under the counter. And it was to this venal industry that the folk song was to be exposed.

The record-buying public of the '20's and '30's was a mixed lot. The upper teens were important, but young-marrieds and middle-agers also contributed to the sales figures. A song became popular after the radio audience had heard it and was interested enough to seek out a recording. Sometimes, a motion picture would bring a song to the audience's attention, and send it into the green pastures of success.

The individual hero-singers became too powerful to suit the record company moguls, and they set up the aforementioned A. and R. men to find new performers and assign them fresh material. This action delivered the industry into the power of a new money-hungry élite —the A. and R. men themselves. When one man is importuned by publishers to use their material and by artists to help them get the big record, it's not surprising that he is the recipient of all sorts of gifts. And while some A. and R. men were capable musicians who were knowledgeable in respect to the needs of the public, some were merely shrewd traders in favors and power. For every Mitch Miller and Henry René, there were many mercenaries who acquired a "piece" of every musical commodity that passed over their desks.

As the audience changed a new catalyst appeared. At first, the disk jockey was a staff announcer who played recordings and old favorites when requested by the radio listeners. But the record-buying audience became younger. More bobby-soxers had pocket money to spend on records and they were more malleable than their elders where musical tastes were concerned. For a while the record program was merely an inexpensive way of duplicating, without remote broadcasting, the hundreds of band broadcasts which were popular on the radio waves. But then the audience began regarding the disk jockey as some kind of superexpert, a being of infinite wisdom and unimpeachable taste. The next day the sensitive song pluggers were parked on his doorstep laden with new songs, new records, and new gifts.

At this point we must again cautiously observe that no song can be played into popularity if the audience doesn't hear something special in the lyric or the music. But continuous presentation of the song does give the audience a greater number of opportunities to hear something special. And so the disk jockey, or "deejay," as he is often affectionately called, helped make hits out of many songs. Since some of these helped start the folk song resurgence, it's important to remember that the deejay is still America's leading musical tastemaker.

Of course, the A. and R. man is still important in programing lesser artists. However, his route of action has changed. Artists who make obeisance to the disk jockey no longer humble themselves before the A. and R. man. So the latter has become a producer. He finds his own artist, chooses the material, pays for the recording and then sells the tape to a record company—often the company for which he worked as A. and R. man. This suits him very well because, despite the diminution in power, it means a diminution in his general income tax payments.

In order to see clearly the power structure in the music industry, so that we can understand what has happened to folk music in recent years, we should follow the progress of a typical song from creation to poplarity.

To begin this odyssey, we must know the source of modern popular song composition. Even the folk song is usually redesigned before it is submitted for publication and hoped-for recording. Who does this job? A decade ago the answer would have been "Tin Pan Alley." This catch-all title referred to the troglodytes who inhabited tiny cubicles in the caverns of Broadway. For the most part songwriters were professionals who appeared daily in the lobbies of the Brill Building or the Paramount Building on Broadway. They worked at pianos and jotted down lyrics on scrap paper, panning away like forty-niners in the hope of one day discovering the mother lode.

Once in a while these men would refurbish an old song and submit it to the publishers. "It Ain't Gonna Rain No More" was a square-dance tune before it became a hit. "Ghost Riders in the Sky" was once "When Johnny Comes Marching Home." For the most part, Tin

Pan Alley produced Tin Pan songs. In Nashville and other Southern capitals, drawling country-music counterparts of the Northern Alley were turning out hillbilly music. Their income came from two sources. First, the publisher paid approximately ten cents for every piece of sheet music sold, and also half of the licensing fee paid by the record company, which was usually about two cents per record. Then there was ASCAP, the American Society of Composers, Authors, and Publishers, which collected money for performances from radio broadcasters and producers. ASCAP would then divide the money with its members—delivering the largest sums to the most active publishers, authors, or composers.

The stakes were high. A hit could sell a million single disks. The writer's share of this would be ten thousand dollars. The sheet music could bring in another ten thousand, and an ASCAP rating five thousand more. Foreign record rights could bring in even more thousands. In other words, the lucky writer could commandeer a lodging on Easy Street for a song.

In 1940, the broadcasters set up an organization to rival ASCAP, which was called Broadcast Music Incorporated. At first BMI licensed only "Jeanie With the Light Brown Hair" and a few others. But it grew into a massive complex as impressive as ASCAP. BMI assigns royalties to composers in direct relation to the performances of their songs logged. ASCAP now has a similar system.

What is this commodity, "the song," which is the business of publishers, record companies, folk singers, and broadcasters? It is a simple collection of musical notes and common words usually about love, organized into "The form." Dean Acheson, a keen observer of the American musical scene, has written. "War songs, marching songs, patriotic songs, drinking songs, songs of old times, songs of laughter and of lament, lullabies, mother and home songs, they can't hold a candle to love." This was true in the past and, despite the healthful injection of folk music into the field, is true today. As one disk jockey bitterly said, "All day long I spin out the whining account of the glories of love at fifteen."

The Popular Song Form is also known as "AABA." If you examine this formula, you will see that it follows the traditional dramatic entities: A^1 is the statement. A^2 is the development of the statement. B, known also as "the release," is the crisis, the catharis, or the high point. A^3 is the coda or closing. Let us make an example of Dean Acheson's last phrase, ". . . they can't hold a candle to love."

A^1: All the things that they teach in schools,
    They can't hold a candle to love,
A^2: All the books and those tired rules,
    They can't hold a candle to love,
B: Give me a chance to show I know
    What I'm speaking of,
A^3: Be my guest, you'll forget the rest,
    They can't hold a candle to love.

The lyric hastily written above answers a number of the needs of the industry and the buyers of popular records. First of all, it is a protest against authority, important from the vantage point of school-age youngsters. It makes a statement in A^1, develops it in A^2, introduces the critical release—in this case, an obvious proposition —and then, using a teen-age slang expression, "be my guest," brings the song to an end. Most popular songs follow this succinct form—telescoping a message as if the composer were writing a telegram. The music is usually very similar in the three A sections, and the B is arranged so that its dominant ending leads us back to the final A^3.

Most folk songs, on the other hand, follow an AAAA-AAAAA pattern. "On Top of Old Smoky," for instance, repeats the melody and pattern of the first verse for all subsequent verses. Consequently, when the folk songs first began to appear in the mart of popular melody, publishers required that "B's" be added to them.

In 1942, I learned at Fort Dix an ancient bawdy song which used in its twentieth-century incarnation the refrain, "A Gob Is a Slob." It derived much of its comic flavor from its AAAA form:

I walked down the street like a good girl should,
He followed me down the street like I knew he would,
CH: A gob is a slob wherever he may be
  Listen and I'll tell you what a sailor did to me,
I walked to my house like a good girl should,
He followed me to my house like I knew he would,
CH: A gob is a slob wherever he may be
  Listen and I'll tell you what a sailor did to me,
I opened the door like a good girl should,
He followed me through the door like I knew he would,

CH: A gob is a slob wherever he may be
  Listen and I'll tell you what a sailor did to me,
I walked up the stairs . . . etc . . . etc . . . etc . . . etc.

As a result of the folk song revival, I was asked for some "folk songs which might become popular." I offered the above retitled, "A Guy Is a Guy." Mitch Miller, an important A. and R. man, agreed that the centuries-old song had merit, but asked for a "B." And so, I interrupted the "A's" with the following:

I never saw the boy before, so nothing could be sillier,
  At closer range
  His face was strange,
But his manner was familiar.

The song was recorded by popular singer Doris Day and was the number one song of the year. I always wonder whether the "release" had anything to do with the success of the old folk tune.

Before publishers will consider a song, a "lead sheet" is usually required. This is a music manuscript which contains the words of the song and a single line of music, sometimes listing the chords by name. Very few publishers will look at a lead sheet, but they require that one be submitted with the "demo," a demonstration record of the material. It is true that there are some publishers and A. and R. men who read music, but they rarely admit to this demeaning activity. They depend entirely upon a performance of the material.

Folk singers, today, gather themselves about a microphone and tape their favorite songs one after another.

Then they send the tape to the publisher. If he is interested in any of the submissions, he asks for a lead sheet and demo. Nonperforming writers usually convince some friend to record the song with simple piano accompaniment. Others may find it necessary to hire some singer who specializes in sight-singing the compositions for a set fee of $15-$25. For some it means bearing the costs of a soloist, pianist, and recording studio.

In some cases, an enthusiastic publisher will hire a whole orchestra and top-notch soloist to make a demo. As folk songs and country songs began to sell nationally, some of these demos became hit records. Many of our thousands of small record companies were amateur recording studios a few years ago. Many of our country and western singers run their own record studios and record their own songs—deriving income as songwriters, publishers, and record companies.

To whom do we bring our lead sheet and our demo? As we can see, the artist who will perform the song often wants to publish it as well. Some artists are not satisfied unless they are credited with having helped to write the material. Even in the case of a folk song, recorded in its traditional form, the artist may feel he is entitled to a share in the composer's royalties. The Kingston Trio assigned "Shady Grove" to their own publishing company "written by Guard-Shane-Reynolds," although it was learned from Jean Ritchie's Kentucky-accented singing. And Harry Belafonte's "Hole In the Bucket" is listed as having been written by Belafonte-Odetta, although the song had been excellently recorded previously, once by Bob Gibson and once by multi-lingual Martha Schlamme. There are legal reasons for this practice which we shall examine in a special chapter, "Folk Music and the Law."

If one cannot reach the performer or his manager or his relatives, there is always the publisher. Publishers, however, will rarely listen to unsolicited material. Too often they have been sued by aggrieved songwriters who claim that some new composition was pirated. Since thousands of songs are written every day, on one subject, using variations of only seven notes, similarity is the rule, not the exception. Nevertheless, a note to the publisher will probably earn you an invitation to submit your song.

If the song catches the publisher's ear, and sounds like the contemporary trend in music, he may send you a contract to sign. Aside from promising the present royalty rate of .04 for sheet music copies, and half of all other money received, he agrees to pay an advance of "$1.00 in hand." In my fifteen years of observing the world of music, I have never heard of any composer's receiving that one dollar bill.

In the old days, the publisher would print copies of the song and send them around to important performers. Today, the publisher mimeographs a few sheets of music but will not "publish" the song unless a commercial recording has been promised. To achieve this moment of euphoria, he calls upon his personal connections in the industry or the abilities of his contact men, the song-pluggers. These men are no longer merely foot-in-the-door salesmen. They know which artist is recording and what sort of song he is looking for. They often initiate song successes by urging staff composers to turn out special songs for special artists.

These men know that there is no use pushing a song at Frank Sinatra the day after a recording session, no matter what the worth of the proffered song. They know that a popular group which has come to town to record a rhythm LP will not listen to the finest ballad. If a singer is told by his agent or manager that he'd better start singing blues songs, he will be met on the street by a group of song-pluggers blessed with what seems like extrasensory perception and a folio of blues songs.

Some managers and A. and R. men have audition periods for publishers. At the appointed hour the publisher or his representative waits outside the great man's office boasting to other publishers or representatives about the "terrific property in this portfolio." Upon being ushered into the presence, they place the great property on the record player. Often it is auditioned for two or three revolutions—a few musical measures. Even if a melody meets with approval, it may never meet with anything else, but remain on the desk with hundreds of other "approved" properties.

In sum, this is the world of music into which folk song has entered. It seems like an impossibility that the simple noise should be accepted by this supersophisticated industry. Why should Jo Stafford and Frankie Laine record folk song albums? Why should disk jockeys feature traditional songs on programs aimed at teen-age urbanites? What started the West Coast production of folk singing trios and quartets?

It is probably true that nothing can stand against an idea whose time has come. Perhaps folk music became a "commodity" for the music industry because it was the time for folk music. But its moment came when an un-named quartet tried to sing like the Almanac Singers, "but with discipline." The quartet later called itself "The Weavers," and it's likely that they were the ones that cranked up the folk song bandwagon.

7.

The Weavers

In his nationally syndicated column, Earl Wilson printed what must have seemed to millions as dogma, "About all you need to be a singer nowadays is a guitar and a cold in the head." The cynic would add, "the cold is absolutely necessary, but the guitar helps." Many articles and polemics have appeared in the public prints concerning rock 'n' roll, Elvis Presley, and other modern musical phenomena. Not many of the critics would be willing to trace these to the success of the four oddly assorted humans known as The Weavers.

In the West Coast folklore publication, *Good News*, Ed Cray ignores The Weavers and ascribes the folk song revival to a series of soirées at the home of Thomas Hart

Benton. At his "at homes" in the nation's capital, Benton played his favorite folk songs on the harmonica, piano, mouth harp, or anything else within reach. Charles and Ruth Seeger, well-respected musicologists, attended a few of these musicales and were enchanted by the vitality of the music, as well as the versatility of the famed American painter.

The Seegers turned to the works of John and Allan Lomax; in fact, as noted earlier, they helped Lomax transcribe his songs for publication. The Seeger children were all inspired to folk-musical heights and, today, have almost supplanted the Lomaxes as "The First Family of Folk Song." In the *Good News* article, Cray calls Peter Seeger the "Pied Piper of Folk Music" and ascribes the present condition of the folk song world to him. We submit that Peter Seeger was an important factor, but he could never singlehandedly have turned the course of popular song. In actuality, he was recruited for help in that task by another giant—large in repertoire, imposing in bulk—whom we have also met earlier —Lee Hays.

Let us remember that in 1946 there were few groups singing folk songs and ballads. Most of the singers were soloists, although the politically minded or religious singers often sang together for spiritual stimulation. There were country and western groups who sang as choruses, but these were considered too "pop" for the folk song fan. However, at the hootenannies most of the folk singers appearing as soloists would sing songs together, in part as a demonstration of the solidarity of the working class. Thus, a very conservative Frank Warner would

have as his mates while he sang his "Tom Dooley" such
fire-breathing left-wingers as Woody Guthrie.

In 1947 there was a hootenanny at the headquarters
of a local union that was located at Astor Place in
New York City. While the program was going on, Lee
Hays sat down in the Union Cafeteria and reminisced
concerning the days when, as an Almanac singer, he
had toured the byways of America. Suddenly, he
pushed his glass of milk aside and leaned toward me
with a very intent expression. Lee is a very large man
and the part of him that was above the table weighed
more than all of me put together, so it was a very impressive lean. "Let's get a group together," he said, "like the
old Almanacs, but with discipline."

I didn't know it then, but I was listening to the stuff of
history. The word "discipline" frightened me half out of
simplicity and I decided to let history take place without my assistance. I explained to Lee that I was doing
very nicely and liked the idea of doing what came comfortably to me without submitting myself to the tastes of
others. Lee looked at me sadly and commented that he
felt that way sometimes, too, but, since he didn't accompany himself on any instrument, he really needed someone else for a performance. We went back to the hootenanny and I forgot the incident—for a while.

Lee forgot the idea, too. However, he continued to
participate in hootenannies and concerts. In fact, he
acted as the mover and doer in a series of intimate fests
held in Pete Seeger's basement on MacDougal Street in
Greenwich Village. Various balladeers would try out
their old songs and some new creations, and the entire

audience, composed mostly of other singers, would join in on the choruses. Among the various balladeers was Fred Hellerman, who began to act as Lee's accompanist and right bower.

Three attractive young ladies of the prebeatnik variety also came by. One, Greta Brodie, had learned many old English songs from her sister, who used the songs for camp entertainments. A second, Jackie Berman, had a large repertory of ballads and Yiddish songs, and later with Bess Lomax wrote her own classic, "The Ballad of the M.T.A." The third worked as a secretary at Columbia Broadcasting System and had a deep husky power-driven voice. Her name was Ronnie Gilbert and, since the girls roomed together, they had the most mellifluous flat in New York City. They, too, would add their voices to Lee Hays' basso, to Fred Hellerman's baritone, to Peter Seeger's low tenor, and to everybody's chorus.

Lee was playing around with musical backgrounds to slide-strip movie films and he had some special lyrics he wanted sung. Consequently, he extracted Ronnie Gilbert from her roommates and used her services exclusively. The resulting sound seemed very pleasant, especially when everyone else at the parties remained silent long enough to listen. Lee began to think again of the Almanacs and the "discipline." They tried singing together for other people's parties and meetings. Fred Hellerman forgot about his banjo-playing—after all, Peter Seeger's banjo was enough for any group—and started playing the guitar exclusively. They were still pretty bad, but they sounded promising.

One day Lee asked if they could appear on my WNYC show as "The No-name Quartet." We offered a prize for a fitting name to apply to the new aggregation. The audience was not completely complimentary and we received a few entries with such titles as, "The Forlorn Four," "The Off-keys," and "The Undertakers." Lee returned after a few more appearances and announced that they had chosen the name "The Weavers." He explained glibly, and without conviction, that they had taken the name because it had a "nice ring" to it, and that, henceforth, they would weave through the warp and woof of American musical life. "I'll take care of the woofing," he declared, "and the others will continue being warped." Later, they admitted that the name derived from the title of the militant play by Hauptmann.

Even with this superior title they did rather badly. They had great enthusiasm but little art. However, after singing a song a few times, they would leave out all the discords and keep in some of the pleasant harmonies. After many programs, the sweet harmonies began to predominate. Some entrepreneurs and party-givers even asked them to return for more singing. At this point, Toshi Seeger, Pete's wife, decided to become their manager. They began to develop a driving sound on their rhythm songs and a gently persuasive quality in their ballads. Ronnie acquired an edge of brass in her voice, which was perfect for blues and gutter-songs. And Freddie began to match Pete in his instrumental versatility.

Toshi spoke to her friend, Max Gordon, proprietor

of the Village Vanguard, avant-garde night club. Max had featured Dyer-Bennet, Burl Ives, Josh White, and many others. The idea of a folk singing "group" was new to him. But he liked Pete's work enough to trust a "Pete plus" arrangement. The skyrocket went up from the Village Vanguard. The audience was stunned. The parties, picket lines, hootenannies, and rallies had so seasoned The Weavers that they were ripe. The agents, producers, and Madison Avenue denizens came rushing out of their offices to spend the night at the Vanguard.

The function of a night club in developing talent and bringing it to the attention of an important audience is extremely important. A performer who appears in a concert is seen by an audience and then goes on to some other hall, usually in some other neighborhood. If the reports are favorable, he may be asked back the next year. There is no longer a vaudeville stage on which the performer may appear day after day, so that the curious may drop by to see what the shouting is about. But when a nightclub act seems special, the word passes quickly and by the end of the first week, the usual inhabitants of the establishment have to stand at the bar while their seats are occupied by very expensive-looking men and women—with great influence in the world of entertainment.

The Weavers didn't stay merely a week at the Vanguard—they were held over for many months. The audience fervor wasn't matched again until years later when Harry Belafonte began his rise to international fame from the same tiny platform. At this point, Toshi

Seeger began to get frightened by the offers pouring in on her four wards, and she looked around for help.

They knew a young businessman named Harold Leventhal, who had been a song plugger for Benny Goodman and Irving Berlin. He brought in a young friend named Peter Kameron who was very well-disposed toward folk music and already knew record company A. and R. men and many popular artists, as well as radio disk jockeys. They gave him the job. As a result of this hand-shake deal, Peter Kameron became one of America's most successful dilettante publishers, Harold Leventhal became one of America's most accomplished concert impresarios, and The Weavers signed with Decca Records.

This was accomplished in traditional fashion. Gordon Jenkins had them audition for Dave Kapp of Decca. Kapp had been associated with Alan Lomax when Lomax first recorded such artists as Burl Ives and Josh White for Decca. He liked The Weavers, and enjoyed their songs, but didn't see how he could get his audience to buy the stuff. Gordon Jenkins tried to change Kapp's mind, but Kapp refused to be swayed by an emotional appeal. Kameron went to Mitch Miller, A. and R. man for Columbia Records. Miller is a believer in "new sounds" and thought The Weavers might catch the ear of the perpetually jaded pop audience. He offered them a recording contract, although with little hope of recouping his investment. The Weavers insisted that Kameron inform Gordon Jenkins of the offer. Jenkins, armed with the tangible evidence of Mitch Miller's interest, persuaded Kapp to record the new group. And Decca Records, whose major artist had for years been Bing Crosby, profited by the acquisition of the innovators and only exploiters of a new popular music craze.

The Weavers' first important record was "Irene" and the billing read, "Gordon Jenkins and The Weavers." Soon they were the featured artists on "So Long, It's Been Good to Know You," which they had learned from Woody Guthrie, "The Roving Kind," which they had learned from me, and "Around The Corner," which they had learned from Josef Marais. Pete Seeger took a short African chant and arranged it into a powerful audience participation number called, "Wimoweh." Lee Hays wrote "The Lonesome Traveler" from a fragment of an old hymn, and then they created "Kisses Sweeter Than Wine" from an Irish lament for a dead cow. Their impact on the world of music was tremendous. Tin Pan Alley was stunned.

The problem of copyright began to plague the group and their publishers. Today there is still a maze of legal twists which do not answer the questions which arise from rewriting or performing what seems to be public domain material. We will try to untangle this mess later on, but at this juncture we can examine the steps taken by The Weavers to protect their songs. Take "On Top of Old Smoky," for instance. It appears in hundreds of collections and in many books as a traditional song. The record company asked for the names of the composers so that they could be paid their royalty fees—and also to protect the record company from accusations of plagiarism. So Gilkyson and The Weavers, under the collective name of "Paul Campbell," applied for the copyright, "as sung and arranged by The Weavers." Later the name "Paul Campbell" became a catch-all for the publisher's folk-type material.

"Goodnight, Irene" was no problem. It had been noted by Lomax in his book about Leadbelly, and it was assigned to him and the Leadbelly estate for Martha Leadbelly, who'd been left penniless at his death. Woody Guthrie was properly credited for "So Long, It's Been Good to Know You." Their big Israeli hit, "Tsena," caused a mountain of trouble. Like many songs from the new land of Israel, it was of recent creation. And some insistent individuals in Israel were each swearing that he was the sole and original composer. Recently Mills Music was awarded the copyright.

"Kisses Sweeter Than Wine" was more intricate, but easier to handle. There is, in Newfoundland, a song which Ed McCurdy had brought back for our enjoyment. It is a half-Gaelic lament to drinnhin dubh, "the dark cow."

Oh, drinnhin dubh, why did ye die?
Oh, drinnhin dubh, why did ye die?
Your back was so black and your tail was so long,
And my drinnhin down derry she ne'er will come home.
Drinnhin dubh lived before she was dead,
Gave me sweet butter to put on my bread,
Likewise warm milk for to stiffen my crown,
But now it's black water for drinnhin is gone.

This song is probably the ancestor to another which has translated the sorrow for the lost bovine into vaudeville bathos:

When the old man discovered his cow it was dead,
Over meadows and ditches and fields then he fled,
Over meadows and ditches and fields that was plowed,
But he never cried, "Thwack" till he spied his dead cow.
Oh, aragh musha, sweeter than thou,
I'd rather lose Patsy, me only firstborn,
Than to lose you, my drinnhin, but now you are gone,
So I must sit down and eat my dry bread,
But there'll be no more butter for drinnhin is dead,
Oh, aragh musha, sweeter than thou.

Leadbelly heard this song from Mary Barnicle of N.Y.U. and syncopated it to match the rhythm of his twelve-stringed guitar. The Weavers wrote new words to the song and made it a love story instead. Because this was a "substantial change," as required by law, the lead sheet bore the imprint, "Paul Campbell."

Kameron and publisher Howard Richmond were rolling along now. With his general manager, Al Brackman, Richmond had helped begin the "disk jockey" promotion approach and the "one big record" drive. While many publishers were trying to get as many "covers" out on a song—recordings of the same tune by different artists—Richmond promised exclusives. He believed that one pilot hit record would bring a hundred imitating "covers." He also made special arrangements with the record companies by which part of his licensing fee would be used for promotion of the song.

Trying to profit from this example, the other publishers began to solicit all the known folk singers for any material which might become popular. Richmond, who had always been partial to folk music, had special rights to Leadbelly's songs, Woody Guthrie's music, Peter Seeger's material, and many others. Josef Marais established his own publishing company. Other publishers began to exhort their regular writers to provide them with "traditional songs."

Paul Cohen, one of America's leading authorities of country and western music, came to see The Weavers and observed to Lee Hays, "You fellows have done something remarkable. Your records are the first big hits which have hit the top on both popular lists and C and W lists. That's amazing—it's never been done before." Until The Weavers it was possible to distinguish between the record audiences for folk-type music and the audiences for popular music. After The Weavers, the barrier went down. All the fans of the great Hank Williams and "brakeman" Jimmie Rodgers came swinging around to push The Weavers' bandwagon. This was music they understood.

Hank Williams had been country music's quasi-deity for years. Part evangelist, part folk philosopher, he was born in Alabama and knew folk music as part of his country heritage. Then he'd drifted into the folk-type field, using hillbilly songs performed with his "Drifting Cowboy" string band. He intoned his way on to tremendous fame as a singer on KWKH's "Louisiana Hayride," broadcasting from Shreveport throughout the South. Finally he was almost apotheosized as the star of WSM's "Grand Ole Opry." He died in an auto accident in 1953, leaving his audience ready for The Weavers' "Darling Corey" or "Lop-eared Mule."

Then there was the Jimmie Rodgers audience. Jimmie was born in 1897 in Meridian, Mississippi. He went to

work on the railroad at the age of fourteen and learned
hundreds of songs, which, like the shining tracks of the
railroad, cut across the provincial boundaries of the
Southland. In his early twenties, stricken with tubercu-
losis, he decided to find rest with a career in show business. As "The Singing Brakeman," he was recorded in
1927 by Ralph Peer for RCA Victor. According to a
recent bulletin from Broadcast Music Incorporated, "He
was among the first to make the nation and the world
aware of the treasury of folk music native to the southern sections of the United States." The Weavers' recordings of "So Long" and "The John B. Sails" raised a
standard that Jimmie Rodgers' fans could follow with
gratitude and enthusiasm.

There was another audience waiting for the magic
touch of The Weavers. These were the former adherents
of the left wing who had turned conservative and were
busy accumulating guilt feelings as Madison Avenue
advertising men, or radio, television, and motion picture
executives. Their espousal of the new group was based
partly on genuine admiration for their stirring sound,
and partly on a nostalgia for the progressive banners
which they had let fall. This was partly due to folk
song's faintly progressive air, and, more realistically, the
result of The Weavers' always including in their program songs with a recognizably liberal message. If In-
donesia were seeking freedom, "Suliram," a simple lullaby, would be performed as a reminder of the struggle. Or Pete Seeger would sing "Wimoweh" with its
nationalistic message, "The lion is sleeping. He shall
awake." There was nothing red-tainted about these, but

compared with the bland diet offered by the pop songs, this was raw meat to intellectuals.

Furthermore, it should be noted that the great Weavers' hit, "On Top of Old Smoky," was a sing-along. The general atmosphere of suspicion and unrest in America had produced a nation of organizations and associations, but few "groups." The stag affair, or the Christmas party, was probably the only conjunction of Americans during which they let down their hair, among other things. But The Weavers, in all their concerts and in most of their records, offered Americans the chance to participate in the emotional experience of group song, and they profited thereby.

In recent years, astute Mitch Miller found further profit in this popular urge. According to the New York *World-Telegram and Sun,* his first thirteen sing-along albums have made over $30,000,000. According to Miller, "The average American has about 3,500 songs tucked away in his memory." At the rate Miller is recording these, the gold mine will have been panned dry by the year 2,500. But by then the audience will probably have tucked away a few hundred more songs. Many of these songs are folk songs, and the audience, therefore, can be expected to enjoy the happy shock of recognition in the same way they enjoyed their first exposure to the songs of The Weavers.

All these special audiences were waiting for The Weavers and their music. There was yet another element, the largest by far. We noted previously that the early records had been bought by young twenties, early thirties, and some late teen-agers. After the Second

World War, the tide turned so that the older groups were starting to turn from popular music, while the younger teen-agers, with extra money in their pockets, began to subsidize the popular record field. Insistent rhythms began to predominate in hit records, and many of the older composers began to complain that their finest songs were not being recorded.

At first, the older society, ASCAP, accused BMI, the new broadcaster-owned licensing company, of skul-duggery. During the recent "payola" investigations, ASCAP declared that payola was a BMI invention to perpetuate rock 'n' roll. But when payola had been scourged and expunged by Congressional pressure, rock 'n' roll records hit new sales peaks. ASCAP, with grudg-ing understanding, is now including rock 'n' roll and rhythm and blues composers in the ranks. "The kids want bang-bang-bang," said a leading publisher, "we'll give them bang-bang-bang. Irving Berlin and Hoagy Carmichael will have to learn to play bongos." The Weavers, emphasizing songs which had been beaten out by blues singers and work gangs, by foot-pounders and square dancers, were ready to meet the new needs. They didn't realize it at first, but they were the wave of the present.

There was one other important element—the long-playing record and the miracle of tape recording. These combined to make possible an inexpensive, sweet-sounding, long-lasting, easy-to-handle record album. It wasn't that way in 1948 when Decca Records asked me to record. Since I was unsure of my singing and my ac-companiment, I refused unless I could have a singing group behind me. I suggested the then unnamed Weavers. Decca pointed out that the expense would be prohibitive. In those days, a record album consisted of six or eight laboriously recorded "sides." Each song had to be recorded perfectly all the way through. Often the artist would perform without flaw and then the engineer would discover that his stylus had over-cut or under-cut the grooves of the master disk. A loud noise or a heavy step sometimes made the cutting head skip or slide. I remember a session in which Josh White was ready to wreck the engineer because a bubble on the recording disk spoiled a perfect take of a difficult song.

When the album sides were ready, they were bound in a heavy cardboard folder containing three or four envelopes. This folder was more expensive than the records. In general, unless the folk singer or pop artist was a sure-fire audience pleaser, the company would hesitate to record him. But then the quarter-inch tape was invented. This was coated with particles electromagnetically rearranged by sound waves, thus memorizing the sound fed to them by the magnetic heads. If a performance was not perfect, the tape could be rerun. If sections of the performance were good, they could be spliced together with no loss of quality. And the resulting sound was better, too.

Since the recording time was speedier, sessions were less expensive for the companies. Besides, an LP album cover was now a simple envelope with a printed sheet or label pasted on it. It was possible to record lesser-known artists without risking much capital. If a singer could promise a faithful audience of a couple of thousand, it was well worth the trouble to put out an album. Small new companies were organized to put out esoteric LP's.

The recent case history of Elektra Records is a fair illustration. In 1951 Jac Holzman, a vagabonding young man, decided to spend a borrowed $200 on a fledgling record company. Some of the new companies were issuing classic jazz performances; others were featuring little-known folk singers. One company appropriately called "Esoteric" was starring the sound of a legendary piano, part of whose legend was the invention of a flamboyant Middle Easterner. Jac Holzman decided that he would risk all with the music of John Gruen.

When the music of John Gruen proved too revolutionary, Holzman began to look for some other way of losing money. Edward Tatnall Canby, distinguished musicologist and sound experimenter, brought Holzman a tape of Jean Ritchie singing songs of the Southern Appalachian Mountains. Holzman decided to issue the record, using his last few dollars and some he borrowed from his twice-touched friends and relatives. Jean Ritchie sold. Holzman decided that folk music had a future—even in 1949. He quickly recorded Frank Warner, Cynthia Gooding, Tom Paley, Hally Wood, Josh White, Ed McCurdy, Sonny Terry, Brownie McGhee, and many others. Weaver Fred Hellerman often acted as music consultant for Elektra sessions.

The tape-recorded LP was so simple to make, so inexpensive to press, that many artists printed their own records. Some universities contributed small sums to issue records based on masters' theses devoted to folk song collecting. Hundreds of singers who would never have been heard outside their farms, towns, or communities, were immortalized on acetate to inspire listeners far out of sight, in settings alien to the imagination of the simple balladeers. In this respect, the work of Kenneth Goldstein is noteworthy for his large-scale presentation of folk musicians on the Riverside, Folkways, and Prestige labels.

To repeat, The Weavers had been propelled into fame so quickly that they never quite understood what hit them. They never really sought the blinding limelight which illuminated them. They accepted the rewards with hesitation and with ceaseless introspective questioning. And when they were finally struck down in full flight by the blacklisting apparatus of the mass communications industry, they may even have been a little relieved—although regretful that their public would be deprived of their spirited wares.

8.

The Blacklist

From the moment when the first draft of a manuscript is typed to the moment when the book is published, many months may intervene. Sometimes, years may pass. If the book is concerned with observations of the contemporary scene, the information therein may become obsolete, the observations no longer appropriate. But of one thing I am sure. When this chapter is read by the general audience, whether it be months or years away, there will still be blacklisting in the entertainment industry. And I am equally sure that folk singers will head the list of those blacklisted.

In the summer of 1951, The Weavers were engaged to appear at the Ohio State Fair. They were then at the height of their spectacular rise—with record after record reaching the Hit Parade. The local Knights of Columbus and the American Legion chapter attacked their forthcoming appearance, citing articles in the newsletter *Counterattack* as evidence. The appearance was canceled and, although the influential *Columbus Citizen* and the *Akron Beacon-Journal* protested, this pattern has continued. According to Merle Miller in the book, *The Judges and the Judged*, "When The Weavers appear in a night club or theater, the management invariably receives at least one copy of an issue of the newsletter in which the quartette has been attacked."

Long before the Ohio State Fair incident, the blacklist was an important factor in the entertainment world. Howard Rushmore, Frederick Woltman, and others of the newspaper fraternity had written several articles after World War II citing entertainers who had sponsored or had appeared before leftist organizations. Militant local organizations followed up these articles with allegations that the persons cited were "unworthy of employment." Of course, this practice was not unknown in America, but it was only after World War II that the list became a bible for show business. Coupled with the rise of folk music was a concerted attack on many of the folk musicians.

We pointed out earlier the extent to which folk music had become a left-sponsored activity in the early days. The singers caroled before Russian War Relief meetings, at Political Action Committee meetings and American Labor Party rallies. Often performers appeared at Communist party functions. A cruel anti-

Communist joke of the period described two party members arranging a meeting, "You bring the Negro, I'll bring the folk singer." Why did the singers appear? Perhaps, some were supporters of the left wing. Usually, it was the promise of remuneration. Sometimes, balladeers appeared at benefit performances in order to keep the good will of the people who provided their bookings. Whatever the reasons, the record shows an uncommon number of folk singers peopling the activities of the left wing.

The songs, too, often seem like left wing propaganda. Many old songs would sound like rabble-rousing pamphlets, even if sung at American Legion conventions:

The general's a dodger, a well-known dodger,
The general's a dodger, and I'm a dodger, too.
He'll march you up and march you down,
Look out, boys, you'll end up underground.

Sidney Hillman once wrote, "It is no exaggeration to say that songs have played a vital part in the upward climb of humanity. Especially this is true about labor songs, which have expressed not only the dreams of an aspiring labor movement, but also have been properly used as a rallying cry to maintain discipline, morale, and high spirits in great moments of struggle." What would our conservative citizens think of a song which complains of the workingman's lot and contains these lines:

They say in Harlan County—
There are no neutrals there—
You'll either be a union man

Or a thug for J. H. Blair.
Oh, workers, can you stand it?
I don't see how you can.
Oh, will you be a lousy scab,
Or will you be a man?

Indeed, what did our conservative citizens think when
the nation sang Merle Travis' popular lines:

Mine sixteen tons and what do you get?
Little bit older and deeper in debt.
Saint Peter, don't you call me 'cause I can't go;
I owe my soul to the company store.

To many members of the fraternity of the press, and
to other important citizens, the early labor movement
was merely an outrageous expression of Communistic
anarchy. Many of the advantages which have been
won for today's workingmen were once considered to
be the goals of Bolshevik slogans. The songs which expressed these aspirations were considered to be
Bolshevik-inspired. Robert A. Juran, writing to *Time*
magazine (January 19, 1962), maintains that the old
labor union songs are now passé. But he avers that a
new type of song has taken their place—about integra-
tion, peace, and the H-bomb. Instead of "The Rebel
Girl," your writer would most likely hear something like
this at a hootenanny:

What will we get from radiation?
No neck, two necks or maybe three.
Each one will have his own mutation,
Nobody else will look like me.

Another reason for folk musicians' being considered wild anarchists is to be found in the personality of some of the leaders of modern minstrelsy. Many of our highest-priced singers practiced their art while leading picket line marchers. Banty-rooster Woody Guthrie walked around with his guitar uncased with the slogan, "This Machine Kills Fascists," emblazoned across the sounding box. Folksy groups sang loud the praises of the CIO, then considered by many as "subversive," or led Henry Wallace's Progressive party in militant melodies. Josh White threw angry songs at his night club audiences, songs demanding immediate civil rights for Negroes. Even Leadbelly, relatively nonpolitical, protested in song "Washington is a bourgeois town," when he found it difficult to obtain lodgings there. If there were any members of the Communist party among them, they didn't show it, for their spirit was strongly anti-discipline, and the backstage scene at a hootenanny was more like a visit to the back room of a bar than a political gathering. Protest was the theme of many of the songs, and the nonconformists who sang them helped create a "wild radical" image.

Despite community disapproval and isolated anti-folksinger manifestations, some of the singers became popular. They appeared on radio shows, in television, in motion pictures, and on the stage. Then, in 1947, the blacklist became an organized reality. In May of that year, three ex-FBI agents, John G. Keenan, Theodore C. Kirkpatrick, and Kenneth M. Bierly, published a newsletter which they called *Counterattack*. Their purpose was "primarily one of accumulating information and files . . . as a sort of research setup for a publication which would be devoted to exposing Communism." The publishing firm was called American Business Consultants.

The Federal Bureau of Investigation frowns upon publication of material in its files. In fact, J. Edgar Hoover has often put himself on record as opposing nongovernmental agencies which are directed against suspected subversion. Consequently, the American Business Consultants depended on the *Daily Worker* and other Communist publications, pamphlets and throwaways from front organizations, the hearings of various state committees concerning leftist activities, the bound volumes of *The New York Times,* and the transcript of hearings of the House Committee on Un-American Activities.

The last-named document had an appendix which, it is said, listed the names of more than 100,000 Americans who, as far back as the early thirties, at one time or another, belonged to alleged front organizations. The "subversives" list was compiled, according to Kirkpatrick, "as a result of photostating all kinds of documents from the New York Public Library: letterheads, notices of meetings, notices of dinners, and all that sort of thing." With these lists, *Counterattack* began to attack persons, especially in the entertainment world, who seemed to have been excessively connected with left-wing causes.

Written by Sam Horn, a free lance who had published several militant articles on the Communist menace, the newsletter was sold through direct-mail solici-

tation and by personal canvassing. Among the first
subscribers were labor unions, clergymen, some government agencies, and a number of business leaders. After
a while the American Business Consultants began to
offer special reports on the personnel of individual companies. This type of solicitation, when coupled with the
possibility of an exposé in the newsletter, made busi-
nessmen eager to subscribe to the reports and to dismiss
questionable employees. In a short while, *Counterattack*
became a rallying point for letter writers and others
whose accusations against prominent entertainers had
been previously unheeded. These accusations became
part of the publication's files.

By 1948 derogatory mention in *Counterattack* was
enough to cause a performer to lose his job. The general
public, however, was unaware of the power of the four-
page publication with the miniscule circulation. Inter-
estingly, the date cited above also marks the beginning
of the decline of the left wing in America. As the blacklist was becoming more potent, the Communist front
was moribund. In the folk music magazine, *Caravan*,
Brown University's Arthur Jordan Field observed, "Interest in political songs and the People's Songs organization began to die out after 1948. . . . The cold war
was on in earnest and what was left of the American
left wing fell apart for more reasons than McCarthy."
Although the publishers of *Counterattack* didn't know it
at the time, they were about to take a stick to a dying
dog.

The advertising trade magazine, *Tide*, quoted a leading agency executive who defended the right of his

profession to question the political beliefs of employees. "Advertising is an attempt to win public support. The use of a means to that end which alienates the support of even a considerable portion of the public is unwise." Events have shown that the agencies and the networks have interpreted a few postcards and phone calls as evidence that a considerable portion of the public is being alienated. Mention in *Counterattack,* coupled with a few letters to the network, usually resulted in the end of a career in mass communications. But this was just a beginning. Soon American Business Consultants provided the entertainment world with an extremely serviceable publication, perfect for organizing a permanent blacklist.

On June 22, 1950, they published the 213-page booklet called *Red Channels, The Report of Communist Influence in Radio and Television. Red Channels* listed the names of 151 writers, actors, singers, dancers, producers, network executives, and others, and coupled each with the alleged Communist-dominated organizations and causes to which they were "reported" to have belonged. The effect of this compilation was immediate and devastating. The lesser luminaries found their workload suddenly lightened. As one actor described it, "It was like that popular song—when I came up for a part I was suddenly either too young or too old."

The situation in which more important figures found themselves was somewhat different. Where the industry had a large financial investment in an executive or performer, massive efforts were made to "get him off the hook." In some cases, the accused met with the accusers and tried to convince them of his innocence. But even if the consultants believed the remonstrations, in most cases it was too late to save the reputation of the individual. The industry's taste-makers all had *Red Channels* in their top drawers; there was no "Review of *Red Channels*" which might correct the errors. Some performers were asked to prove through some militantly anti-Communist act already performed that they were no longer sympathetic with the radical left. One important folk singer told a press conference that he had been "a dupe" for racists. Another presented his informal jury with a list of forthcoming benefit appearances for right-wing groups.

The general public did not know about the blacklist until, in August of 1950, the Jean Muir case hit the country's headlines. Advertising agency publicists at Young and Rubicam announced that former screen star Jean Muir had been chosen to play the role of Mrs. Aldrich in the popular Aldrich Family television show. Miss Muir was one of the 151 listed in *Red Channels,* and *Counterattack's* Kirkpatrick telephoned "two or three people" to apprise them of the agency's decision. One of those he called was Mrs. Hester McCullough of Stamford, Connecticut. Mrs. McCullough had just successfully defended a libel suit brought against her by Paul Draper, the dancer, and harmonica virtuoso Larry Adler, both of whom she had accused of being "pro-Communist."

Mrs. McCullough also "called a few people." Among these were Stephen Chess, Queens Commander of the Catholic War Veterans, "a man on the Americanism

Committee of the Connecticut American Legion, and a couple of women I know on Long Island." She also called the National Broadcasting Company, which had contracted to broadcast the Aldrich Family series. Her call was followed by another from Rabbi Benjamin Schultz, Executive Director of The American Jewish League Against Communism and coordinator of The Joint Committee Against Communism in New York. Rabbi Schultz told the network that Miss Muir should not be permitted to appear and concluded, "I am speaking for the more than two million members of my organization."

No one checked Rabbi Schultz' figures, but Jean Muir did not appear on the Aldrich Family show. The sponsor, General Foods, issued a press release stating, "The use of controversial personalities or the discussion of controversial subjects in our advertising may provide unfavorable criticism and even antagonism among sizable groups of customers. Such reaction injures both acceptance of our products and our public relations. General Foods advertising, therefore, avoids the use of material and personalities which, in its judgment, are controversial." It is evident that, swayed by this doctrine, folk music and folk musicians would be seriously affected by the blacklist—including musicians not even listed in *Red Channels*. We have already discussed how, by the nature of its content, folk music excited controversy, and how most folk musicians began as nonconformists.

In a speech to the Radio Executives Club on October 19, 1950, Theodore C. Kirkpatrick remarked, "I don't say you shouldn't hire the performers listed in *Red Channels*. I do say that those who continued to support Communist party causes since June 23, 1950, must take the consequences." However, the radio executives and the agency men adhered to the tenets so clearly stated by General Foods. For the most part, they never questioned whether the 151 listed had stopped supporting the Communist fronts, or whether, in fact, any were pro-Communist. All were, by virtue of the listing, too controversial for employment in mass communications.

The blacklist increased in size and potency. Vincent Hartnett, former naval intelligence officer and television supervisor, had written the introduction to *Red Channels*. He placed in the *Brooklyn Tablet* an ad stating that "*Red Channels* was a piker." This was to publicize his own *Confidential Handbook*, which listed many names not in *Red Channels*. In 1952 more names were added to the list by the Senate Subcommittee on Internal Security, chaired by Senator McCarran of Nevada. Many of these new names were supplied by blacklisted performers and executives seeking "clearance." Among these were some of America's finest folk singers.

Our leading balladeer asked to testify, explaining that his presence at leftist meetings did not mean that he was affiliated with the Communists, and the same was true of the hundred or more he had named. He expressed regret at having to name these others, but declared, "I will have to do it because these people will have to do what I have done, and many others. They will have to make up their minds on this matter."

Despite this disclaimer, the mere mention of a name at the Senate Subcommittee hearing was enough to make its bearer unemployable. The only road to "clearance" for those named was a trip to Washington, an appearance before the Subcommittee, and the naming of a few other suspects. Such a public act of contrition did not guarantee a return to the fold. In fact, proof that one had never been a Communist sympathizer didn't often help. One remained "controversial" once he had been named in connection with the Communist conspiracy.

As the *Saturday Review* pointed out, in commenting about *Red Channels*, "To accuse is enough." Today, in broadcasting circles, a few letters will cause the dismissal of a minor actor or official. A major letter-writing campaign may end the career of a topnotch star. Of course, this will be effected in a very subtle fashion. The network will issue a publicity release proving the allegations false, and then, at the expiration of the actor's contract, drop him because his rating is down, or the time spot is no longer available, as was alleged in the John Henry Faulk case.

Television producer David Susskind began his illustrious career with little prior knowledge of the power of the blacklist. In *Show Business Illustrated*, January 23, 1962, he describes his experiences: "We screened not only actors for their political affiliations and backgrounds, but also every member of the crew: engineers, audio men, lighting men, directors and writers." Since a mistake would offend the blacklisters and cause the executive in charge to be suspect himself, the anxious entertainment moguls turned for help to the blacklisters. Susskind continues, "It was general practice for an agency to subscribe to a service which, for a fee, would check the 'Americanism' record of any actor, technician, director, or writer. This fee ranged from $10 to $25."

The blacklist even extended to suspected songs. In 1946 a West Coast newspaperman wrote a talking-blues called "Old Man Atom." The theme of the song was, "All men can be cremated equal." The conclusion was:

Here's my thesis,
Peace in the world,
Or the world in pieces.

Columbia Records bought the rights to the original West Coast recording, and RCA Victor brought out its own version of the song. Both of these disks were doing very well until shortly after the Jean Muir case. Then, in August of 1950, the Joint Committee Against Communism, still "representing two million members," informed the record companies that it considered the song subversive. They insisted that the lyrics parroted the line of the Stockholm Peace Petition, which they claimed was being circulated by Communist sympathizers. The song was immediately withdrawn by the two record companies and was banned from the airwaves.

The Weavers were the special target of the blacklist. The late Howard Rushmore, in the *Journal-American,* reported with approval that the quartet had been prevented from appearing on the Garroway telecast because of "the appearance of The Weavers at Communist functions and the frequent listings by Congressional

Committees of Pete Seeger." Pete Seeger left The Weavers and his place was filled by talented, respectable, unlisted Erik Darling, but The Weavers were still prohibited from network television and radio. On January 4, 1962, they were scheduled to appear on the Jack Paar evening telecast, emceed by Sam Levinson. The afternoon of the taping, they were requested to sign a loyalty oath and refused, declaring that it was demeaning. They did not appear.

This loyalty oath is now often used by the networks. It was originally introduced by CBS in 1950 as a statement that the prospective employee was not now and had never been a member of the Communist party or of any Communist organization or Fascist group. This early CBS oath required that the signer declare nonmembership in over two hundred groups designated by the Attorney General as "totalitarian, Fascist, Communist, or subversive." Membership in People's Songs was enough to cause doubts of one's patriotism. As a consequence, many incipient folk singers had to try to live down the taint of their subscriptions to the *People's Songs Bulletin.* Since most of the well-known singers were already blacklisted, the industry had to look to new faces for its stars. Where these people came from will be the subject for the next chapter. But first, I think it important to express an opinion concerning the merits of blacklisting.

I'm sure that the reader is already aware of my feelings on the subject—my treatment of this matter is hardly unbiased. It is possible that I am one of the few performers extant who was blacklisted by both the left and the right. I was among the chosen 151 listed in

Red Channels for having appeared before many front groups as an entertainer. Since I had never been favored with the confidence of the left I was unable to "clear" myself by naming acquaintances or pertinent facts before the investigating committees.

The reason that I am now working for the networks, major industries, and even governmental agencies, is the result of a happy discovery by the House Un-American Activities Committee. According to Mrs. Monti, one of their chief investigators, a number of former Communists had testified in secret session that I had been blacklisted in 1946 and after for having refused to perform for Communist party programs. My refusal was based upon some unpleasant experiences at leftist programs where I had been admonished for singing songs contrary to that week's party line. Since I had no access to the constantly changing policy of the Communists, I decided to forego their contributions to my income. My relationship with People's Songs deteriorated and I asked that my name be taken from their masthead.

My prejudice against blacklisting, then, is highly personal in nature. But it is shared by some notable men, including playwright Elmer Rice: "I have repeatedly denounced the men who sit in the Kremlin for judging artists by political standards; I do not intend to acquiesce when the same procedure is followed by political commissars who sit in the offices of advertising agencies or business corporations." Fulton Lewis, Jr., the Mutual network commentator, had himself been under extreme pressures for his right-wing broadcasts, but he spoke out against the blacklist of the suspected left, "I am against any listing of names that is used to force people out of jobs. But even more than that, the whole listing in that book was done without any of the proper kind of investigation. Why, we do more research for a single broadcast than those boys seem to have done for the whole book."

It is generally presumed by right-thinking men in the entertainment world that the blacklist—and certainly *Red Channels*—is no longer operative. This is self-delusion. The week before I began this chapter I was called by the producer of one of television's most important shows, a man of remarkable integrity. He informed me that mine was one of many names which had been turned down by "Continuity Acceptance" for an appearance the following week. The others rejected never knew the reason for their nonemployment—an atomic scientist had signed an anti-H-bomb petition, a singer had a blacklisted brother—but I was able to meet with the legal department and call to their attention the minutes of the House Committee. When it was demonstrated that my anti-Communism predated that of most of the blacklisters, the doors were again opened to me. I was informed that their rejection was based upon my appearance in the now dog-eared, tattered pages of *Red Channels*.

How many folk singers appeared before left-wing organizations without espousing their aims? How many refused to testify or sign loyalty oaths because such actions seem humiliating? The Weavers' letter to Robert Sarnoff said, in part, "We deeply resent the indignity that such a request implies. Moreover, we feel very strongly that no private business establishment such as NBC has the power or right to require proof of any citizen's patriotism and certainly not the right to act as an arbiter in such matters." It made no difference. As Raymond Gram Swing pointed out in a speech to the Radio Executives Club in New York, "A person once named, however innocent he may be, can never quite be rid of the taint . . . the taint, not of his guilt, but of his having been named." Our society was founded to protect the innocent, even if ten guilty men were to go unpunished. If it is possible that one innocent man has suffered, the blacklist is reprehensible.

The above is not a popular doctrine. When Jack Paar returned to his show after The Weavers incident, he warmheartedly confessed that he really didn't know whether it was just for a performer to be required to take an oath of allegiance. The *Toronto Telegram* (Jan. 19, 1962) commented on Paar's dilemma and complimented him on his bravery. "This was a case in which the safe and easy thing to do would be . . . to endorse NBC's stand. His failure to do so will probably get him on a couple of 'lists' himself."

Should a blacklisted performer be allowed to appear before an American audience? The blacklisters believe that the suspect's appearance on national broadcasts adds to his prestige. Thus the performer's backing of left-wing functions and policies will carry more weight. Secondly, they point out that the more money the blacklisted performer makes, the more he can spare for Communist causes. And finally they say that it is only fair that individuals with well-known anti-Communist records should be used in preference to those whose sympathies are in question.

Theodore Bikel, accomplished actor and leading folk musician, wrote on behalf of the Arts Chapter of the American Jewish Congress, "We, as artists, must protest an act that seeks to compel the performer to bargain for his livelihood with other values than his talent." The American Civil Liberties Union has stated that, apart from positions importantly affecting national security, "Employment should be decided on the basis of qualifications strictly relevant to the particular task involved."

Some people believe the blacklist is unworthy of notice. But this book would not be complete without a discussion of a subject which has so greatly influenced the world of folk music. I say let the actor play his part. Let the singer sing his songs. Surely our people are proof against propaganda from the left, as they have always refused to be stampeded to the right. How many fine songs and stirring performances would have been lost if our maligned singers had not been allowed to sing? It is a frightening thought. But even if the blacklist were to strike down only a few untalented performers I would be against it. Blacklisting is a despicable art.

9.

In the Wake of
The Weavers

Time magazine's music editors noted in an article on
the new "folk music boom" that The Weavers' success
"has made them the most widely imitated group in the
business." However, the next important phenomenon,
after The Weavers' rise, was the ascendance of a solo
performer. In 1948, while The Weavers were busy
amassing an enthusiastic audience, I was asked to stage
the Town Hall presentation of "The Lonesome Train."
This moving work, which tells the story of Lincoln's
funeral cortège, had been written by ex-Almanac singer
Millard Lampell, with music by another intimate of the
Almanacs, Earl Robinson. Robinson was to be the nar-

rator for the production, and the CIO Chorus was to be conducted by another folksinger, Robert DeCormier.

In the middle of our harried, hurried rehearsals, De-Cormier approached me, almost tearfully, with the tale of a recalcitrant performer who was making his work impossible. This young man had been hired to sing the stirring sermon of the preacher, a powerful evocation of the grief of the Southern Negro upon learning of Lincoln's death. The performer was insisting that it was not necessary to learn the role. DeCormier insisted that the part be committed to memory. It was a dangerous stalemate.

The young performer was Harry Belafonte, a painfully handsome actor who had been singing popular songs and blues with minor success. Belafonte's voice was chronically hoarse as a result of improper placement, and the husky quality, coupled with his moody male beauty, had gained many fanatical adherents. In fact, he had opened a tiny Greenwich Village hamburger shop in the hope that these fans would support him with their patronage.

While DeCormier listened with annoyance, Belafonte explained that he felt it unnecessary to learn his part since the presentation was in cantata form. Besides, he pointed out, very accurately, he wasn't getting enough money to warrant memorizing a musical work he'd probably never use again. He was incensed, furthermore, that he was required to give an explanation for his decision. It was obvious that Belafonte felt that non-Negroes were ganging up on him. I tried hard to reach him through the wall of hostility, to convince him that I respected him as a man and as a performer. And I pointed out that he could never do justice to the wild fervor of the preacher's lament if he were bound to a printed script.

Belafonte is a very perceptive man and a very proud one. He is also a remarkable showman, well aware of the power of his own physical grace. I'm sure that he was already aware of the truth of DeCormier's position but couldn't bring himself to an admission of agreement. He seized upon one of my tangential comments concerning the inadequate lighting at Town Hall and turned to DeCormier asking him, "Why didn't you mention that the lighting was bad?" DeCormier preserved a dignified silence. As a footnote to their early mutual antipathy, it should be revealed that DeCormier later became Musical Director for Belafonte.

The Town Hall production was a huge success and Belafonte was a powerfully frenetic preacher. He incorporated part of the sermon into his popular song programs and looked about for more material with the same folk quality—especially songs which presented the Negro in a dignified role. Some of these he borrowed from Bob DeCormier's folk song repertory, but that was limited. Then he began to hear of Huddie Ledbetter, "King of the Twelve-Stringed Guitar." Before he could meet Leadbelly, the great singer died of a withering bone disease. Once again, New York's Town Hall stage played host to folk musicians, when, on January 28th, 1950, a Leadbelly Memorial Concert was arranged by Alan Lomax. The variety of musical styles was a hint of a future confluence of folk and pop music. Woody

Guthrie sang duets with Tom Paley right after Hot Lips Page and Sidney Bechet blew some wild jazz riffs into the rafters. Pete Seeger led The Good Neighbor Chorus in a program of folk songs, and W. C. Handy followed with a few of his original blues. Jean Ritchie quietly strummed her Kentucky dulcimer with a goose quill and then left the stage to Count Basie and his real gone piano. Tom Glazer sang some old ballads, the Lord Invader jangled some calypso tunes on a West Indian cuatro, The Weavers sang "Irene," Reverend Gary Davis raked the audience with his crude gutter gospels, and Bill Dillard's band jazzed from one side of the stage to another. There was genial Frank Warner singing a few songs from his special, private collection—songs like "He's Got the Whole World in His Hands" and "Tom Dooley." Finally, Leadbelly's close friends, Sonny Terry and Brownie McGhee, joined Sticks McGhee in some sophisticated blues.

Leadbelly was dead, but his songs were on the open market. Belafonte found a special personal excitement in the musical charades and powerful songs of the grizzle-haired illiterate with a frightening prison record. Today, Belafonte's repertory is a distillation of the spirit and material presented at the memorial program at Town Hall. In fact, American music today is almost a direct reflection of the kind of amalgam which Town Hall provided that night—blues, ballads, calypso, and jazz mingled in what is now popular song. When we listen to the street gospels of Gary Davis, we find ourselves surprised by the sound of the '60's—rock 'n' roll.

At first Belafonte tried to mix a few folk songs into

a popular program. Then he began to dispense with the pop songs, which seemed pale next to the full-fleshed traditional material. He decided not to hamper his physical movements with an accompanying instrument —and left the guitar harmonies to Craig Work, a descendant of one of America's most respected musicologists. At this point, Jack Rollins, a very astute performer's representative, recognized in Belafonte and his repertory the strange stuff from which a national idol can be fashioned. He booked him into the Village Vanguard and invited the press and producers to view his "discovery."

Belafonte went up like a missile. His personal beauty and the smoldering quality of his angry personality added to the drama already present in the songs. The cult spread like a religion. One day while preparing an LP for Victor Records, he was introduced to a quiet, scholarly composer named Irving Burgie. Burgie had made a study of the calypso style, and with Louise Bennet, a wonderfully talented West Indian woman, he had toured the folk song circles as "Lord Burgess and his Serenaders." He showed Belafonte some of his rewrites—"Jamaica Farewell," "Linstead Market," and others. Belafonte was enchanted. He discarded the songs he'd already prepared for recording, and made a calypso album instead. It was one of the first longplaying albums to sell over one million copies.

An appreciation of Belafonte in *The New York Times* observed that he "uses the near-hypnotic pose of a male fashion model, setting up a curious type of body tension that fascinates an audience much as a flame fascinates a moth." Let us add to this our belief that Belafonte would have scaled the heights no matter what material he chose. The quality of stardom can rarely be denied. However, it was the onrush of the folk song tide that moved him ahead so quickly and deposited him on such a high pedestal. In turn he made millions of people more familiar with the sound we call folk music.

Hundreds of imitators appeared, most of them only briefly. But much more was required of the performer by the American audience. Johnny Horton managed a few folk-type hits such as Jimmy Driftwood's lyric to an old fiddle tune, "The Battle of New Orleans." We've already mentioned the performance of the latter-day Jimmy Rodgers, who hiccoughed "Kisses Sweeter Than Wine" into prominence again. Tennessee Ernie successfully essayed Merle Travis' "Sixteen Tons." And there were others with little influence.

Of course, young Elvis Presley is the exception. His performances of the Negro-influenced Southern country music revolutionized our music industry. Presley was not, as most critics believed and hoped, a flash in the pan. Without much vocal ability or musical know-how, he projected a pulsing animal vitality into the national popularity sweepstakes. Campaign-managed by an inordinately skilled medicine showman, Colonel Parker, he helped spread the gospel of rock 'n' roll. Since his training reflected the Southern concatenation of country music and gospel shouting, it helped make the folk sound more palatable generally.

The next important folk music outburst was the result of a group endeavor. Shrewd entrepreneurs, emboldened by the success of The Weavers, had tried all sorts of combinations to capture the Weaver audience. At first, it was considered imperative that a folk singing group be composed of one woman and three men. None of the organizers could imagine that some other combination was possible. Sometimes, they turned to genuine folk artists for the nucleus of such a group. Jean Ritchie was recruited for one. So was Hally Wood, a young lady from Texas who had absorbed the traditional style while transcribing melodies for Alan Lomax. None of these experiments turned out to be a "second Weavers." The magic formula, it seemed, wasn't to be found in numbers or quality—it was to be found in the spirit with which the folk song material was presented.

During this period, The Weavers continued to be an important factor, despite their being blacked out on radio and on television. They were especially popular on college campuses and were continually booked for university programs despite the objections of local blacklisting authorities. Even more important, their records were prized in every fraternity house and dormitory in the country. And, as has been mentioned earlier, the development of the LP was a tremendous vitalizing factor for American folk music. Many formerly unrecorded singers appeared on record, and small record companies began to invade the college market.

Soon alongside The Weavers' albums and the Harry Belafonte albums were set albums of ribald songs, ancient ballads, and hymns of protest. It became possible to travel from a campus in Maryland to a campus in Southern California and hear students sing the same

New England version of "Cape Ann"—copied from a Richard Dyer-Bennet or John Jacob Niles LP. As the collegians began to trade songs and join in harmony, small on-campus groups began to form. Some of these gained local popularity and began to think in terms of national fame in the manner of their common idols, The Weavers.

For instance, there were two young men who went to Punahou High School in Honolulu. They strummed the ukelele in typical Island fashion and developed a comic diving act which was very popular for a while. One of the two, Dave Guard, enrolled at Stanford University. The other, Bob Shane, went to Menlo Park Business College. It was here he met Nick Reynolds, who had drifted up to MPBC from San Diego. The three young men tried singing together after college and found the sound they made not unpleasant. Since Belafonte's Burgie-inspired calypso album was the rage, they decided to adopt a West Indian title, "The Kingston Trio."

At first, in their own words, "We batted around some college hangouts singing for cakes and coffee." Then a clever manager, Frank Werber, appeared and "he really put us through the hoops. You listen to your voice on tape, you go to a vocal coach, you practice on your instruments, and eventually you don't sound quite as bad as you did." Then, as Bruce Cook describes the result in *Rogue* magazine, "The story of their success is straight out of Horatio Alger, as edited by Madison Avenue. . . . There is no long drawn-out history of small-club dates and waiting for the 'big break,' no list of sleazy hotels and a diet of canned spaghetti warmed over a smuggled-in hot plate, no brush with the law or even a hint of a management link with the Mafia." The Kingston Trio were on top.

Their songs were copied from records of folk performers, often with the regional accents. Nevertheless, Dave Guard reported, "When we find something we like, we adapt it. It may not be ethnic when we get through with it, but after all—what is ethnic? Why should we try to imitate Leadbelly's inflections when we have so little in common with his background and experience?" The Trio's use of other singers' material has resulted in many legal tangles, but most observers will agree that they have shown excellent taste in their choices. That their success is not a fly-by-night manifestation has been shown by the continued sale of their records. Hundreds of imitators have appeared and disappeared, proving that the original had a very special quality which is not easily copied.

In 1960, *Time* magazine quoted the Trio as saying, "When we fight nowadays it's mostly about business— what to invest in." *Time* added, "The Kingstons get along remarkably well." In 1961, Dave Guard left the winning combination after a bitter fight. The West Coast folk song magazine, *Good News,* attributed this to Guard's being "fed up singing the same damn songs over and over again." Whatever the reason, he has set out with a new group called, "The Whiskeyhill Singers." Since Capitol Records has an interest in the title "Kingston Trio," the remaining members of the trio recruited young John Stewart of The Cumberland Three to take Guard's place.

The Cumberland Three was one of the many groups organized to profit from what seemed like a landslide. "The Ballad of Tom Dooley" hit so hard that the music world was stunned into recognition of certain inescapable facts. The Weavers had done it. Belafonte had done it. And now a few college kids had done it. These were not isolated phenomena. Others could do it, too, with the proper folk songs and suitable musical drive. Besides The Cumberland Three, there were The Chad Mitchell Trio, The Gateway Singers, The Limeliters, The Dauphin Trio, The Wayfarers, The Travelers, The Tarriers, The Babysitters, The Balladeers, The Folk Singers, The Brothers Four, and countless others.

Some had relatively minor success. The Tarriers recorded "The Banana Boat Song" and an altered version of a George Sea Island chantey:

Pay me, oh, pay me,
Pay me my money down,
Pay me or go to jail,
Pay me my money down.

This they sang as "Cindy, Oh, Cindy," and found themselves riding high. But, unable to repeat their success, they were forced to sing on the sidelines while the newer Kingston Trio won tremendous rewards. Erik Darling, one of The Tarriers, finally took Pete Seeger's place on The Weavers' roster, then left his place to Frank Hamilton, brilliant Chicagoan. In similar fashion, Lou Gottlieb of The Gateway Singers joined Alex Hassilev and Glenn Yarbrough to create The Limeliters. The Limeliters achieved their successes by their clever

musical arrangements, their highly intellectual intro-
ductions, and a deal with Victor Records in which a
portion of their royalties was to be used for publicity.

The Brothers Four were also West Coast collegians—
their title is derived from their being members of the
same fraternity. They use cymbals and bongo drums to
back up their songs and harmonize in simple cherubic
style. Their material is a mélange of folk music and
popular songs with folk-type leanings. They have no
screaming fans, but depend for their success on record
hits such as "Greenfields," "The Green Leaves of Summer," and a cheeky parody on "Frog Went Acourting"
called "Frogg":

Frogg went acourting and he did go, uh huh,
To the Coconut Grove for the midnight show, uh, huh,
Minnie Mouse was the hat-check girl, woo, woo,
He thought he'd give this chick a whirl, woo, woo.

One college-bred trio turned their backs on this type of
song for Bluegrass—The Greenbriar Boys. Some turned
their backs on the middle of the twentieth century. The
New Lost City Ramblers decided that they would seek
inspiration from those early recordings made in 1926 by
Riley Puckett, Uncle Dave Macon, Frank Hutchinson,
Tom Ashley, and such groups as the Buckle Busters,
and Dr. Smith's Champion Horse-Hair Pullers. Peter
Seeger's half-brother, Mike Seeger, is a Rambler. So is
Tom Paley—the young man who sang with Woody
Guthrie at the Leadbelly Memorial Program. The third
of The New Lost City Ramblers is a Yale graduate
named John Cohen. John learned his folk music early

in New York City from his brother Mike (one of a group known as "The Shantyboys"). John remembers that back in 1952, when he was a freshman at New Haven, "most Yale students considered folk singers left wing, out group, and odd scene."

At first, John recalls, only a few art students and graduate students from the math department sang folk songs. Then others began dropping by until two or three hundred students were showing up for hootenannies. Yet, "the hoots were not really respectable. We heard of actual fist fights, held in dormitory rooms, where students tried forcibly to prevent their roommates from going to the hoots—on the grounds that it would seriously impair their future chances, particularly for government jobs, if it were known they associated with people like us." Of course, this situation has changed. The Weavers, The Kingston Trio, Belafonte, The Brothers Four, and others have made folk music relatively respectable.

Unfortunately, college students who come to the newly acceptable and highly popular folk singing field believe that the Kingston Trio is the fountainhead of true folk music. In 1961, I was the organizer of a nation-wide Goya Guitar contest on college campuses for folk music talent. Group after group, singer after singer, reproduced the songs and performances of the latest Kingston Trio success. It was as if there had never been a Leadbelly, a Jean Ritchie, a Samantha Baumgartner, or an Aunt Molly Jackson. The college trend seems to be toward duplication of the efforts of The Brothers Four and other similar groups. These groups, I must mention, are quite valid as far as I am concerned, but it would be a shame if their sophisticated styles blanketed out creative folk singing of a less collegiate nature. A possible antidote lies in the person of sultry Mexican-Irish-descended Joan Baez. Joan appears at college campuses driving a monogrammed hearse. She has achieved what one observer called "a sensational oneness with the college students of our country." She has a sweet clear voice and an understanding of the old songs. Her popularity may help extend undergraduate awareness of folk songs and folk singers.

Another exception to the rule of the Kingstons is the popularity of Theo Bikel. A wise performer and highly respected stage and motion picture actor, Bikel brings to his material a dramatic flair which has delighted full houses in concert halls and university theaters throughout the United States. He sings in seventeen languages, and convinces his listeners that each is his mother tongue. Recently released from his daily starring role opposite Mary Martin in "The Sound of Music," Bikel has more time now to exert his influence on our budding folk singers.

From Alabama has come Odetta Filious Gordon. Odetta, a trained singer, states that she is "not really a folk singer except where it comes to gospel songs." Like many of our leading exponents of the art, Odetta began to sing folk songs while she was living on the West Coast. She found a large audience while singing at the Gate of Horn in Chicago. Now her audiences cheer her from seats in halls in almost every state in the land.

Of course, there are still available for programs such

consummate artists as Sonny Terry, Brownie McGhee, Frank Warner, Jean Ritchie, Jack Elliot, and many others. One night, while I was running a concert for the State Department at Cooper Union's Great Hall, Alan Lomax came by with a "new discovery." Her name was Bessie Jones, and Alan claimed that she was "worthy of the mantle of Leadbelly, Woody Guthrie, and Molly Jackson." The audience agreed—and cheered the clear-voiced singer from the Georgia Sea Islands until the recording engineer pleaded that the volume was bending his indicator needle. With such singers active and willing to sing, it may be possible to extend the horizons of some of our Kingston-minded folk fans.

Recently, Mike Seeger's sister, Peggy, returned to the United States from extensive world travels, bringing with her Ewan MacColl, whose records had already had a fair popular vogue. Audiences were treated to some fine British singing, performed by a man who rewrites much of his material with the skill of a poet, and presents his ballads with a fine acting instinct, acquired during years of theatrical performance. After touring the United States and Canada for a year, MacColl returned for a short visit to England. Because of some of his left-wing utterances, his reentry was blocked and American audiences will have to content themselves with his stirring recordings. Already his influence is being revealed on campuses where young people are singing Scottish ballads with newly acquired burrs.

Further signs of hope for variation in presentation come from the country music artists. There's always Earl Scruggs or Lester Flatt, virtuosos of the strings with

Bluegrass music. Once in a while, a hit record comes from the Cockney sparrow, Lonnie Donegan, which reminds us of our own American heritage. Many singers learned about Leadbelly from Donegan's imitations.

But, even if the Kingston Trio is overpopular, it's important to remember that they exist because of The Weavers. As we stand here surrounded by thousands of new folk singers, we should realize that they come in a direct line from the group which, for political reasons, still stand as prophets with little profit in their own land.

10.

Washington Square

When professional folk singing was still a fledgling art, and Leadbelly, Guthrie, et al., were the chief practitioners, newcomers could test their wares at political parties, rallies, and picket lines. As these functions began to go out of fashion, the folk singers looked for a new spotlight in which to shine. Undergraduate folk singers were able to use fraternity club rooms and dormitories. Stars had their great concert halls, or intimate nightclub stages. But novitiates had nothing, except for a few private parties. New institutions were necessary. In New York City, two were developed to meet the need. The first was the fountain at Washington Square. The second, the Village coffee house.

Washington Square, of course, predates even Henry James. It is a cameo park, approximately eight square blocks, with a few playgrounds for Greenwich Village children, and concrete walks for local strollers. There are a few grassy plots about, but they are very unconvincing. At the northern, Fifth Avenue, end is a small replica of the Arc de Triomphe, used mainly as a terminal marker around which the Fifth Avenue buses crepitate to change direction. In the center of the park is a circular walk surrounding a concrete pool with a fountain, used during the warm summer months as a wading pool for children and exhibitionist adults. As it is the tradition in the American Southwest for young people to walk the "paseo," around the town center, so Greenwich Villagers amble around the fountain on sultry Sunday afternoons.

"The Village" in New York City is a remarkably complicated idea. Many taxi drivers will refuse to ferry passengers into its weird reticulations. Once a collection of private farms, it is now a maze of disordered streets—where, for instance, 4th Street crosses 12th Street, 11th Street, and 10th Street before its "One Way West" signs become "One Way East" signs. It has two private newspapers and one of the world's greatest concentrations of foreign cars outside of a foreign country.

The Village is that seacoast of Bohemia in which Millay reclined, lighting candles at both ends. A few yards from the park, Eugene O'Neill staged some of his revolutionary plays, and Maxwell Bodenheim walked nightly with disordered sheaves of foolscap under his arm. It was the ruffled nest from which the off-Broadway

theater was hatched and is a center for dissidents, rev-
olutionaries, crackpots, and innovators. But it is also
the site of one of America's most conservative populations, which bitterly resents its gypsy neighbors. The
Italian-descended residents of Greenwich Village enjoy
a cold war with the free-living, free-loving artists and
the tourists that infest the streets every evening of the
week. The Italian population, however, draws its own
audiences, who want to see the pushcarts which line
Bleecker Street in the early afternoons, or participate in
the pageantry of the Italian street festivals.

Besides these two antipathetic populations, there are
hosts of ex-suburbanites recently fled back to the stimulation of urban life, there are old settlers who labor
honestly in Village shops and factories, and, of course,
there are the working poets, writers, artists, and actors.
Some of these live in ridiculously overpriced apartment
houses—the rents are the highest in the city—while
others live in unbelievable cold-water flats complete
with sagging ceilings and unwanted animal life. Some
live in apartments which were once stables or carriage
houses. Some live over the girly shows on West Third
Street, or the genuine beatnik cafés on MacDougal
Street.

In the middle of all this phantasmagoria is New York
University, Washington Square Branch. It is one of the
largest and most respected institutions in the country.
For years the University has been acquiring property on
Washington Square, buying up the lovely little houses
that front on the park. Little by little these graceful townhouses have become offices, fraternity houses,

study halls. In this way, the University has acquired for its students a very pleasant campus—Washington Square park. On school days they hurry across the Square, past the chess players, past the baby carriages, past the lovers walking hand in hand or arm on waist, and past the bearded, sandaled beatniks. Despite the variety of types inhabiting the Square, one wouldn't necessarily predict an explosive situation. But there has been explosion upon explosion. The Washington Square folk music riots were only one series of incidents in a continuum of raw-nerved conflagrations.

In the mayoralty of Fiorello H. LaGuardia, New York City was at its most honest and most moral. The Little Flower was a reformer of the Carrie A. Nation school. With characteristic flamboyance he swung the axe upon gamblers, tin-horns, and street peddlers. He instituted hundreds of ordinances dedicated to the welfare and morality of the city and its residents. One of his ordinances prohibited unlicensed street musicians. No longer would the booming trombone herald the approach of the German street band. No more would the many-hued parrot pick fortunes from off the top of a hand organ. The hurdy-gurdy was escorted off the sidewalks of New York, along with the accompanying monkey and mustached operator. Many New Yorkers protested, but LaGuardia was unmoved. The nights were no longer to be filled with music, except for too-loud radio programs, or the sounds of off-key whistling in the dark.

In 1945, according to the legend, a commercial printer

named George Margolin raised his voice in song while walking around the fountain in Washington Square. In those days, the buses were allowed to drive into the park and puff their carbon monoxide at the old trees and denuded lawns. Despite the sound of their massive motors, the folk music of Margolin persisted and was heard above the whine and bluster. The next week, the printer brought his guitar along and made more music. By the third Sunday, there was a small audience waiting. A month later, other folk singers decided to take advantage of the listening throng. In a few months, singing at Washington Square was an old tradition.

Americans like to create old traditions. If a publicity agent one year asks the men of a town to wear beards for the centenary celebration, they'll probably insist on wearing beards every year at the same time. America is full of even less extended traditional groups, like "The Monday Bowlers," or the "Five Thirty Poker Commuters." Somehow the singing of folk songs in Washington Square provided the Sunday crowd with a tradition that seemed to provide echoes of Valley Forge, and Bull Run, of Johnny Appleseed, and the Old Chisholm Trail.

For the most part, the songs were Burl Ives-Woody Guthrie-Leadbelly staples—"Irene," "On Top of Old Smoky," "Betsy From Pike," and "Careless Love." The singing continued into the quiet hours of the evening, although some of the singers took time out for lunch, supper, or simple snacks from the ice cream wagons. Those were very happy times. The crowds got bigger and bigger. More and more folk singers joined the group. The music became louder and more spirited. The local residents began to complain.

In the case of the folk musicians, the police believed they could act with impunity. There was no folk music lobby, nor, at the time, was there much political or national interest in traditional song. Deferring to the wishes of the old residents, the police began to enforce the LaGuardia ordinance. As one officer pointed out, there were other good reasons for stopping the songfests:

1. The singers are making too much noise and disturbing the neighborhood.
2. The large gatherings are attracting hoodlums, perverts, and riffraff.
3. Extra police have to be assigned to street gatherings, and the police force is undermanned.
4. Many of the singers are communists.

After many Sundays of interruptions and arguments, two young singers named Jean and Joe Silverstein applied for police permits as required by law. At first there were adamant refusals. Then there were postponements and delays. The applicants persisted and demanded that the license be granted in the spirit of the law. Finally, the permit was granted and the singing sessions became legal assemblies. Of course, this provoked the anger of the old residents and the pressure was once again applied to the "finest" and to the Park Department.

A careful reading of the license enabled the police to ban all but ". . . a string instrument." At first, the songsters debated whether to use a guitar or a banjo. Some said the guitar was more flexible, others said the banjo was louder. A few dissidents recommended a string bass, and one even devised a "Brownie bass," using a wash-tub for resonance, and a broom handle along which the single string could be stretched. While the debate was still going on, the license applicants merely applied for a certificate with broader allowances. This was granted, and once again banjos and guitars rang out on the Square.

Then the police limited the number of participants. The first comers were allowed to sing, the late ones were urged to move on. When this proved difficult, the police tried to divide the crowd into smaller groups. Instead of one large community sing, small knots of soloists, in-strumentalists, and group singers spread around the water fountain. The Park Department decided to limit the time for the singing—from a 2-to-8 session, it was narrowed to a 2-to-6 affair. No one was happy with the strictures, and the old residents kept complaining about police laxity.

Nevertheless, the music was a Sunday delight for hundreds. Tourists came visiting on buses, subways, and motor scooters. Walking about the fountain, they shopped from one musical group to another. Here was a calypso band, complete with steel drum, over there were Bluegrass groups, banjoists facing each other with fixed stares plucking out identical melodic runs in the style of Earl Scruggs, patron saint of the clan. Quiet singers, who dared to imitate the already passé singing style of Burl Ives, had little vogue, because it was impossible to hear them above the general din. The folk singers had brought to the Village the rich cacophony formerly associated with an oriental bazaar.

Some of America's finest and best-known singers live in the Village, and so there were many Sundays during which The Weavers, Theodore Bikel, The New Lost City Ramblers, The Tarriers, Jack Elliott, Woody Guthrie, and many others joined the singing. As the good word spread, visitors came from all over the world to listen and trade songs. And although the acoustics left much to be desired, and the audience was perambulatory, many young singers perfected their art in the bedlam of Washington Square. The trouble with the Square was the short duration of the police passport to pleasure. Where were these singers to go before and after the licensed hours? And was there to be silence in the City during the other days of the week? And what was to become of the songs when the leaves began to fall into the fountain and the permits failed them?

Where there is a need, a solution is generally called for and the answer to the folk singers' dilemma was soon supplied. The old residents—let them rend their clothes if they will—had themselves provided this solution; the coffee houses were the next stop on the road to frequent folk singing. The coffee house was once an important British institution. Lloyds of London, for instance, was at one time merely a coffee house in which insurance brokers sat among their own kind. There were special coffee houses for literary people, like those favored by Samuel Johnson. And there were coffee houses near the Thames for naval persons. In one of the latter, Captain

Isaac Hull, master of the U.S.S. *Constitution* wagered a hat that his ship was superior to that of Captain James Dacres, master of the H.M.S. *Guerrière*. Later, when England and the United States were at war, the two ships went sailing after each other on the high seas, like two wrestlers sidling around a prize ring, just to settle a wager agreed upon in jest at a dockside coffee house.

In this fashion, Americans learned of the advantages of the British coffee house, and in 1737 the Merchant's Coffeehouse was opened for American business. The institution flourished for a while and then fell into disuse. Then in 1935, Dominick Parisi imported a genuine espresso machine into Greenwich Village. The genuine espresso machine is a wonderfully impressive boiler, which looks like a Rube Goldberg creation. Nowadays, the machine is designed in "juke box moderne," a fantastically tasteless chromium calculated to capture attention even in unlit rooms. The sound of the genuine espresso machine is indescribable—a ghastly retch.

The machine at the Caffè Reggio cost $2,000, without cream or sugar. But Parisi recouped his investment in a short while, vending coffee and leisure to the Italian-Americans of the South Village. They appreciated the gurgle of the espresso machine, the click of hot coffee cups upon the marble-topped tables. They came to enjoy a game of chess or checkers with old friends, or to read the Italian newspapers which earlier visitors had left on the ice-cream parlor seats. The Reggio and later coffee houses were havens from the haste of urban life.

Up to this time, Americans had nothing to compare with the sidewalk café of Europe, or with the continental coffee house. In our large cities, there is usually some cafeteria which stays open all night, and there the intellectuals, dissidents, and insomniacs congregate, uncomfortable in the glare of fluorescent lights reflected on antiseptic white-tile walls. Should some night owl raise his voice in song, he would find himself expeditiously guttered, after having been urged through the usual revolving door. There are plenty of bars available, but in America, except for a few hangouts for the literati, the saloon is not a place for intellectual stimulation, for sober reflection, or for the singing of anything except "Adeline" and "I Had a Dream."

College campuses are often blessed with a good beer joint, in which one beer entitles the purchaser to a few hours of singing and noisy ruminations. But beer often provokes unpleasantries and headaches. The universities desperately needed the coffee house, and David Grossblatt recognized the possibilities of the situation. Grossblatt was an artist who had spent much time in Europe. He felt that the coffee house was too good to be limited to foreigners and opened the Café Rienzi, just down the block from the Caffè Reggio. The Rienzi was no intimate room—one hundred and fifty customers could enjoy their cappucino at one sitting. The menu was elaborate—with café mocha, café royale, café viennois, café rom, even café americaine. There were plenty of checkerboards available, as well as daily newspapers of all political persuasions. And soon there were plenty of customers to fill the one hundred and fifty seats.

At such close range, even less far-sighted entrepreneurs could see the advantages of the coffee house.

More were opened for business, serving cider and pastry, with young actors and actresses as short-order chefs and waitresses. And there they waited—these new establishments—for the next chapter in our story. This began the moment that a few of the disappointees from Washington Square came wandering along MacDougal Street or across Bleecker, banjos and guitars slung over their shoulders.

At first, the proprietors of the coffee shops prohibited any singing or playing. Many had installed high-fidelity equipment which transmitted Bach and Pergolesi through the coffee-scented air. But a folk singer is usually compelled by nature to sing folk songs, and one did. Others joined in. Coffee drinkers turned to watch and listen. Chess players even smiled a bit over their checkered battlefields. A new audience had been born. The word spread among the folk singing fraternity that a perfect platform for new songs and new singers had been discovered. In Sausalito, Pasadena, San Francisco, and Los Angeles new establishments appeared bearing such names as the Unicorn, the Garret, the Ash Grove, the Troubadour. In Philadelphia the Second Fret; the Exodus, The Tarot and The Spider in Denver; The White Horse and The Door in Seattle; The House of Seven Sorrows in Dallas;—they were springing up like dragon's teeth near colleges and universities everywhere on the American Continent, each complete with appended folk singers and their audiences.

In Greenwich Village, the Rienzi was followed by the Café Wha, the Lion's Head, the Fat Black Pussy Cat, the Figaro, and tens of others. There were even places

where the folk music was featured instead of the coffee
—at the Bitter End, or at Gerde's Folk City—one half a
bar, one half a hootenanny. Saturday nights in the Village became a pub-crawl, except that coffee was served
instead of alcohol. The streets were thronged with mo-
bile Villagers and invading tourists. All this was anathema to the conservative Village residents who watched
bitterly from their windows. Their weekends became
technicolor nightmares with folk music scores.

To add to their horror, they observed the influx of
bearded young ascetics who walked their streets on
sandaled feet. They couldn't conceal their distaste as
long-haired girls paraded the Village, dressed in the
new uniform of nonconformism—black leotards and
formless sweaters. They were stunned by such libertine
sights as homosexuals walking hand in hand. And—
this is probably one of the major causes of Village tension—they glowered at the sight of Negro boys walking
with white girls, or Negro girls hand in hand with white
boys. Isolated fights began to break out on Sullivan
Street, Thompson Street, and in the park. On a few
occasions, the police were forced to clear the park at the
approach of dusk. Real estate owners began to complain
of the violence and carnival atmosphere. University
officials asked for better policing. Again pressure was
brought to bear on politicians. And again, folk music
was cited as the villain of the piece.

The police began to issue summonses to the coffee
houses. In some cases, they cited the coffee houses for
having folk singers in as "entertainment," a title which

would have caused angry denials in the City Council. "If you have entertainment," said the police, "you are running a cabaret. You must obtain a cabaret license." Not only is this an expensive procedure, but it is a long-drawn-out one. Entertainers, even teen-age folk singers, are required to have cabaret permit cards. And the Municipal laws prohibit "entertainers" from mingling with patrons of the "cabaret." An attempt to clear the way through this morass of regulations could easily unseat the mind of the coffee house proprietor. The tribulations of Kafka's Joseph K. were as nothing compared with a trip into the New York City Municipal Code.

While the authorities pressured the coffee houses, influential members of the community protested to the Department of Parks. When the delegation of folk singers appeared, guitars in hand, to apply for their monthly licenses, they were rebuffed. It was explained that they were ruining the grass in the park and causing an immigration of undesirables to the scene of their singing. The folk singers decided to defy the authorities. The next Sunday they gathered in force, armed with guitars, banjos, Brownie basses, mandolins, and recorders. They were led by one Israel Young, proprietor of The Folklore Center, a MacDougal Street clearinghouse for records, books, and public notices about the folk music world. Young's emporium had been for years a nonprofit enterprise as a result of his too-easy credit terms, his beneficent sponsorship of concerts, and his low resistance to hard-luck ballads sung by needy musicians. He spoke to the crowd, requesting them to sit around the fountain, without singing, in order to bring their cause to the attention of the expected press and television agents.

It was a warm Sunday afternoon. Police were thickly stationed in the park. They wanted no trouble. At first, they tried to move the demonstrators out with courteous shoves. The crowd moved turgidly, and so those left in the rear were vulnerable to most of the shoves. Some of those shoved turned back and protested. This led to more shoves and a few pokes. One hothead even went so far as to swing at a policeman. A few of the finest hurried over to subdue the swinger. A few folk singers hurried back to help their comrade. More police arrived. Someone began to sing.

We're fighting for our freedom,
We shall not be moved,
We're fighting for our freedom,
We shall not be moved,
Just like a tree that's standing by the waterside,
We shall not be moved.

From the middle of the crowd, a banjo picker began to play the chords to accompany the singing. A guitarist joined in. According to the law, singing wasn't illegal, but playing an instrument without a license was. The police, pawns in a struggle not of their choosing, were ordered to prevent this brazen disregard of LaGuardia's Law. And so they attacked the folk singers, who were in like manner pawns in a struggle not of their choosing. To the great delight of the television and newspaper reporters, a mêlée ensued directly in front of their cameras.

The riot at Washington Square was featured on all the networks and carried by all the press services. The European journals ran delighted articles about the revolutionary students of Greenwich Village, and readers smiled tolerantly, remembering their own student days. In Europe, revolutions always began on the campus. In America, public sympathy was with the folk singers too, but not because of our revolutionary tradition. It is probable that the current popularity of folk music is what saved the day for the Washington Square singers. With few exceptions, the rest of America rallied to the defense of free song.

The next week it was announced that a special street, adjoining the park, would be roped off for folk singers. "Here," said the police, "you may sing whatever you wish—and it will keep you off the grass." Since the fountain area in Washington Square is concrete paved, this must have puzzled many, but they gathered in the side streets by the dozens. On nearby corners, eager for the chance to wield a few blows against these "un-Americans," were groups of local teen-agers, glowering at the sight of beards and banjos, mandolins and Negroes. There would certainly have been violent clashes had not the crowd been laced with scores of plainclothes men. These appeared with remarkable agility wherever a minor scuffle occurred, and they jostled the hostile participants apart. So the first Sunday after the riot was a draw, except that the folk singers managed to sing into the network microphones a few telling songs, including two composed by Lee Hays:

Wasn't that a time,
Wasn't that a time,
To try the souls of man;

and

If I had a hammer,
I'd hammer out love for all my brothers
All over this land.

After a few weeks, it was decided that licenses should be granted. Washington Square was once again the province of Sunday singing. The coffee houses began to fight back, too. A few proprietors complained in court that a few venal policemen had tried to shake them down for bribes, and that some firemen had been asking for "ice," too. The charges were not proved, but the angry resistance made the coffee houses a somewhat "hot" item, a little too warm to manhandle comfortably. Besides, the lawyers for these spunky little establishments began to attack the legality of the "cabaret laws," and pointed out that these were set up to regulate liquor-serving salons, not coffee cafés. Soon the coffee houses were again filled with music, one advertising, "Ten folk singers, no waiting."

And so Washington Square and the coffee houses mirrored the nation-wide trend. In this contemporary success story, young people end up in nonalcoholic surroundings, and listen to folk music instead of smutty jokes in off-color cafés. It is probably true that there are unpalatable hangers-on fringing the coffee-society set. There may even be some anarchists and sexual deviates among the throng. But it is doubtful that they wield much influence. Perhaps, some of our fallen citizens may be redeemed by the sound of folk music heard above the bird calls of Washington Square. The Salvation Army doesn't have the monopoly on stirring anthems. Perhaps, the lesson of Washington Square may help bring folk music to the public parks of other cities and towns, and coffee houses to the Main Streets of the world.

11.

The Censors

In the murk of a coffee house or the sunshine of Washington Square, each fledgling folk singer reaches the moment when he must program a public performance. From that time on, he must contend with the major problem of censorship—political censorship, economic censorship, and bowdlerization. But perhaps the most important of all is the self-censorship which results from the desire to be loved and highly remunerated. This last is usually the least mentioned, although the most effective censorship of all.

Let us say that a performer begins his career with a repertory of x number of songs. He performs a program and discovers that his favorite ballad has a dying fall when performed as an entertainment. It is very likely that he will put his favorite ballad away and try his second favorite. In this way, he allows the audience to censor his material. We pointed out earlier that the folk singer often appeared for left-wing causes in the early days. Consequently, many folk singers, seeking a crowd-pleasing roster of songs, discarded many of the non-political ditties.

Audience expectation is a very important part of entertainment. Many singers are afflicted with the necessity for appearing on a "folk music variety show," such as a "hootenanny." If a famed singer is the star, they assume that the audience has come to hear the type of material associated with the famed singer. It is not unusual for the second-string singer to favor material which he thinks will prove particularly palatable to the first-string singer's audience. We do not say this is a good idea—"be thyself" is our own motto—but we have noticed this kind of self-censorship in many concerts.

Similarly, a singer who has had some success in rural areas finds that city audiences lean to a more staccato type of humor with the comedy snapper at the very end of the verse. Often, he will either discard the songs that are too leisurely, or rewrite the verses to fit the needs of the metropolitanites. In constantly rewriting and discarding material in order to suit what he believes is the need of his audience, the artist is performing an extensive censorship of his own material.

Of course, external censoring is more dramatic and deals with more interesting areas—for instance, the ribald, the political, and the discomfiting. For an example of the latter, I well remember W. Colston Leigh, director of an important lecture agency, warning me against repeating the errors of a well-known balladeer. "He was the kind of man who would sing Easter songs for the Hadassah, and Israeli marching songs for the Moslem League."

There are ample possibilities in a folk singer's rounds for performing "inappropriate" material. One famous trio were censured for singing "Frankie and Johnny" to a kindergarten audience. And, while you can sing children's songs for adults, it is unwise to perform them for teen-age sophisticates. The nine-year-old also resents any material which sounds like "kid stuff." Similarly, a men's discussion group in a small town becomes enraged if the program is too lively and entertaining. Mr. Leigh of the lecture agency has a letter in which a Tennessee town protests the excessive humor of a folk song program as ". . . more like a women's club speaker."

The question of good taste is of vast importance in this area. A singer who is asked to perform on a program in memory of some revered figure would do well to eliminate the inconsequential and vulgar from his list. And a folk singer asked to fill in the moments between rowdy cheering at a football rally should consider performing rousing participation material rather than an extended version of "The Death of Queen Jane."

Political censorship is, of course, an important part of our daily life. And it has been one of the important factors in the shaping of the world's folk music since man first began to sing. Here we come to a remarkable contradiction: protests can be more effective when presented as songs, yet protest songs are often allowed where printed disapproval is censored. For the best example, we need only turn to the thousands of slave songs which spoke of freedom in areas where such sentiment was anathema to those in power. Many people would say that the slaves disguised their longing in various ways, thus hiding their feelings under such masques as:

When Israel was in Egypt land—
Let my people go.
Oppressed so hard they could not stand—
Let my people go.

or

Joshua fit the battle of Jericho
And the walls come atumbling down

or:

Master's gone so let him rest;
They say such things is for the best,
But I won't forget till the day I die
My master and the bluetail fly.
Jimmy crack corn and I don't care,
My master's gone away.

Chain gangs have produced many songs with such loudly intoned lines as:

If I was sure the guard was blind,
I'd leave this dusty road behind.

or

I thought last night the good Lord said,
Drop your chains cause the captain's dead.

Sailors of earlier years, who served under a mono-
lithic command more tyrannous than any on land, still
managed to join in many virulent choruses:

Bully Hayes he loves us sailors,
Way, hay, roll and go,
Yes, he does, like hell and blazes,
Way, hay, roll and go.

And the rule-bound Navy managed a few too:

The enlisted man eats in the wardroom;
The admiral won't eat with the mob.
It ain't that he eats any better;
He don't want us to know he's a slob.
The enlisted man rides in a motor launch;
The admiral rides in a gig.
It ain't that he rides any better,
But it makes the old bugger feel big.

And, of course, the Army is notorious for its lese majesty:

The sergeant, the sergeant, he is the worst of all,
Wakes you up in the morning before the bugle call;
Squads right, squads left, squads form into line,
Then the lousy son of a b, he gives you double time.

I'd rather be a private of the lowest class
Then be a lousy sergeant and kiss the looey's brass.

or:

When the war is over, no more will I roam,
Unless they make me General so I can stay at home.

All these, it may be argued, were being performed on sufferance in the expectation that such singing would act as a safety valve. And, possibly, the chanteymen and the angry young singers were allowed to perform their antiestablishment songs so that the establishment could thus parade its own leniency in such affairs. In like manner, totalitarian governments often allow hostile writers to perform within their boundaries as proof of their forbearance.

Whatever the reason, sometimes the folk songs have helped provoke and exploit powerful opposition. The Irish Rebellion was nourished and maintained by a constant diet of new poems and songs. The French Revolution needed "Ça Ira" and the "Marseillaise." And British democracy owes some of its development to such songs as "The Cutty Wren." The wren, among the peasants, represented the Barons and the land-owning clergy. It is believed that "John the Red Nose" in this medieval song was a leader of the peasant rebellion:

"Will you go hunting?" says Milder to Malder.
"We may not tell you," says Festle to Fose.
"We'll hunt the Cutty Wren," says John the Red Nose.
"We'll hunt the Cutty Wren," says John the Red Nose.

"What will you do then?" says Milder to Malder.
"We may not tell you," says Festle to Fose.
"We'll cut her to pieces," says John the Red Nose.
"We'll cut her to pieces," says John the Red Nose.

"What will you with them?" says Milder to Malder.
"We may not tell you," says Festle to Fose.
"We'll give them to the poor," says John the Red Nose.
"Give all to the poor," says John the Red Nose.

Despite the fact that some of these protest songs were tolerated, we need not point out that it has never been the custom for singers to perform antiauthority songs in the teeth of the authorities. And in many countries, the authorities show their teeth wherever the arts exist. Furthermore, as we stated in the chapter on the blacklist, the folk singer who would like to be successful in the mass media must reject, in selecting his material, songs which might prove offensive to the powers that be. Since the powers in our own society are concerned with protecting the sponsors from any unpleasantness, this means a sponsor-centered programing of folk music presentations.

The above refers to the singers who have achieved national recognition, with the exception of Peter Seeger. Harry Belafonte often sings anti-Jim Crow material but when Harry sings "Let my people go," it becomes exciting entertainment rather than propaganda.

There are some who say that "American folk song is democratic," and that "A folk song is a song concerned with the interests of the folk." Therefore, they deduce that it is really impossible to present a "folk song program" without trumpeting antiestablishment doctrines. There is, I believe a demonstrable fallacy in this hypothesis. The interest of the folk often lies in simple entertainment. There is enough material available to popular singers for them to record hundreds of LPs without ever singing a nonconformist line. Furthermore, a slight change in a word or phrase may exorcise the political curse in a directional song.

Yankee, Russian, white or tan,
Lord, a man is just a man.

becomes:

Black or white or red or tan,
Lord, a man is just a man.

In some songs, such as "The Dodger Song," if a scurrilous verse about "the candidate" or "the general" should offend, one need only pluck it out—leaving scurrilous verses about lawyers, doctors, lovers, merchants, farmers, and even balladeers.

The result of this continuous winnowing is a body of material performed in the concert halls, on records, on radio and television, and, consequently, in colleges and at private gatherings, which is not a true representation of folk music. Experts will answer that there have always been two bodies of folk song existing side by side, the public art and the private material. But until mass communication, the same audience was able to enjoy both bodies of material during the same era, the kind of selection depending on the situation of the performance.

Today because of the previously mentioned sensitivity of the mass media, the areas allowed expression in folk music have been excessively narrowed. Organizations and fraternal groups have given way to pressure groups. Trade brotherhoods have become lobbyists. Songs about racial groups or immigrants may bring recrimination upon the singer.

The following are some examples of public disapproval with my WNYC programing which caused various mayors of New York City to reprimand and caution me. Soon after World War II, a distinguished figure in the literary world, William Cole, volunteered to sing on my program some Nazi Army songs, which he had learned as one of our conquering soldiers. These he sang in German, after an introduction describing how old songs had been rewritten by the Nazi troops. Even today such material could hardly be presented on the air as historical material. At that time, I almost lost my program as a result of public outcry.

During the Bay of Pigs incident in Cuba, CBS news offered to lend me a monitored broadcast from Havana which contained some songs of the Castro forces. I jumped at the chance and broadcast these on my WCBS "World of Music." The phones began to ring with complaints before the material was eight measures old on the air. Similarly, a broadcast on which I played some anti-Castro material was greeted with letters accusing me of "imperialist warmongering."

A few years ago, two young journalists presented, on

my WNYC show, recordings of the Algerian rebel forces, made at great risk in their mountain hideout. Of course, these songs immediately brought accusations of "Communism" and "un-Americanism." On another occasion, I introduced some wedding music from a recording of Cantonese street songs. This was proof to letter-writers that I was in favor of Mao and ready to sell Formosa to the Chinese Reds.

Two days before writing this paragraph, I received a letter which commented on one of my NBC-TV "American Treasure Chest" programs. There were five children on the show, one of whom was a Negro. I had been warned that this might prevent syndication in the South, but I hadn't expected Northern hostility as well. The letter in question accused me of "advocating racial intermarriage." I would not, as have many influential producers, equate one letter with a majority opinion. But this type of pressure, especially when channeled through letters to higher-ups, can influence one's future decisions considerably.

Once I sang a silly ditty I'd learned in Minneapolis:

My name is Yon Yonson,
Ay come from Visconsin,
Ay vork in the lumber yard there.
Ven I valk down the street all the people I meet
Say, "Hey, you. Vhat's your name?"
And I say,
My name is Yon Yonson,
Ay come from Visconsin . . . , etc.

Cards and letters of protest were sent to the Mayor's office. It was William O'Dwyer who forwarded these to me with the notation, "Please explain these." The writers called me a racist, a snob, and even an antiunion extremist. But New York's Director of Communications, Seymour N. Siegel, a man of remarkable integrity, refused to be pushed. In fact, WNYC has maintained many other folklore broadcasts, including those by Henrietta Yurchenco, Jackie Sharp, Eithne Golden, Pru Devon, and wandering microphonist Tony Schwartz. An ingenuous disbelief in my own potential for exciting people was my only defense. But, constant pressures from one side or the other will inevitably result in a folk song repertory as watered down as the soup described by Woody Guthrie as "so thin you could read a newspaper through it."

Let's just try one more example from "The Kansas Boys" to show how the mass media operate on folk song material:

When Kansans go to meetings, the clothes that they wear
Is an old gray coat all ragged and bare,
An old straw hat more rim than crown,
And a pair of dirty socks that smell the year round.

Suppose I am asked to sing the song on a network show. My first job would have to be persuading the Kansas viewer or listener that this is not an anti-Kansas movement. I might point out that the song is sung in Kansas as "The Nebraska Boys." But, it is more likely that the continuity acceptance department would insist on more drastic measures. In this case, I am fortunate enough to know another version of the song entitled, "The Good-for-Nothing Boys." But by the time I produced the new version, the continuity department would wearily have suggested a completely new song— and mumbled something to the producer about getting hold of a singer who doesn't come up with so many headaches.

Another important field for censorship is the broad panorama of ribaldry. It doesn't play much of a role in broadcasting where even the word "hell" is unacceptable. But what a shambles is made of the claim that concerts, books, and records are "representative," when bawdy material is excised. This is not an especially contemporary problem. It has been with us as long as folk music has existed.

Such literary treasures as *The Canterbury Tales,* Shakespeare's plays, and the Bible give some indication of the once free expression of what are now called "obscenities." In private company and in small social groups, the four letter words and racy bawdiness persist. But rarely on the public platform does one hear about "The Jolly Tinker Who Came From France" or "The Ball of Kerrymuir." And, since the public is of the opinion that these are "dirty," they are often used by nasty-minded people to befoul rather than to amuse.

One would assume, after examining hundreds of folk song collections, and after playing hundreds of LPs, that there are no bawdy songs in the American song bag. But this is terribly untrue. The reasons for this misrepresentation are many. First of all, state law prohibits publication of "obscene" material. And even the Supreme Court's statement that material becomes obscene only when it appeals to "prurient interests" has done little to change this situation. Secondly, the readers are often incensed against publication of ribaldry—wary of sensationalism and fearful that the collector is trying to subvert their innocent children.

Often, the collector never hears the bawdy material because of the reticence of the singer. And even if one does discover such songs, self-conscious puritanism may cause the collector to rewrite the material. For one of these reasons, the great British musicologist, Cecil Sharp, spent much time revising ancient lays. James Reeves' book, "The Idiom of The People" contains many of the original lyrics collected by Sharp, such as "The Foggy Dew," "Gently, Johnny, My Jingalo," and others. And a later Reeves study, *The Everlasting Circle*, performs a similar task with the extensive works of Baring-Gould.

Last summer we drove up into the beautiful countryside of the French Maritime Alps, where lives Gershon Legman, embattled against the authorities of the world, master of ribaldry, enemy of prudery, and lover of the open word. He described his long efforts to gather together a scholarly, carefully documented study of ribald song. He has been harried, insulted, starved, and assaulted, but he persists. Before we left, he promised that his definitive volume on the bawdy song would soon be forthcoming. We wonder. Of course, if it is to be printed, it will have to be in France, which allows anything to be published, as long as it is not printed in French.

When I was collecting songs of the armed forces, I wrote to a noted midwestern scholar requesting assistance. His answer was friendly, but he observed, "There are very few real folk songs available in that category. Most of the material is just dirty." For this collector, and many like him, I would recommend the reading of W. Roy MacKenzie's *Quest of the Ballad*, in which he observed: ". . . no popular version of any sort of ballad, ancient or modern, can be regarded as common or unclean."

The bawdy song, like the bawdy story, has always been with us. But it is not for this reason that we deplore the censorship of ribaldry. After all, war has always been with us too, and we would not, therefore, support its continuance. No, we are in favor of the free currency of the bawdy because they are often healthier expressions of man's animal vitality than much of the self-conscious literature which enjoys free rein in our culture. In his introduction to *Bawdy Songs*, Louis Untermeyer observed: ". . . The men who first made them . . . composed their rough rhymes not furtively, but with forthrightness, with simplicity and naturalness. It is a kind of innocence that considers no subject indecent or taboo and that assumes the same acceptance on the part of the listener. . . ." The performer of the bawdy song must always present his material with good humor and with freedom and gusto. The moment he, or his audience, begins to regard the songs as "dirty," a disservice is done to the spirit of the material. Unfortunately, censorship does not analyze the intent or effect, it operates automatically and mechanically emasculates our folk song repertory.

Naturally, the most dramatic censorship is found in

the political song. A recent article in the *This Week Magazine* quoted Mitch Miller as having compiled a hit parade of Soviet popular tunes—actually copied from a Soviet catalogue. These included: "The March of the Physical Culturists," "A Wedding in Our Dormitory," "The Song of the Happy Tourist," and "The Celebrated Tractor Driver." These were certainly amusing and illustrative of the Communistic approach to any popular art. But how does our democratic product compare? Where are our anti-administration songs? On how many programs have songs been sung with the sting of "90 Cents Butter?"

When you go to ask them the cause of it all,
They hand you a line about ten foot tall,
They moan and groan and tear their hair
About the high cost of being a millionaire,
Take a full page ad in the Evening News
And blame it on Negroes, Reds, and Jews.
Well, I was born in the bushes and raised in the woods;
They can't sell me that line of goods,
'Cause with 90 cents butter and 90 cents meat
How in the world can a poor man eat?

Here again audience expectation does the nasty trick of equating protest with un-Americanism. I'm sure that a few readers of this chapter were shocked by the above verse, although its expression is a reaffirmation of the constitutional right to disagree with the temporary powers which rule our nation. How many singers would venture to perform this kind of material before audiences which recoil from such political statements?

It is to the credit of our democratic way of life that

the censorship of folk music and popular song is not being perpetrated by the government or by any official agency. It is a pity that American audiences, displaying narrow-minded disapproval, have themselves whittled down the possibilities of stimulation and entertainment. Our frontier heartiness has fallen before the orderly canons of conformity. We are the censors.

12.

Singing Servicemen

The kind of censorship described in the last chapter applies mostly to civilian life. Where the armed forces are concerned another set of rules applies. There is no taboo on the wildly bawdy in the barracks. Since griping is a respected custom, there are plenty of antibrass and antiadministration songs.

According to Harold L. Peterson, of the Company of Military Collectors and Historians, old China hands in the Marine Corps used to sing:

From the coasts of Venezuela,
To the Southern China Sea,
We fight for U. S. Steel,
And the oil fields of John D.

We battle for the DuPont boys,
We make the Morgans rich,
And if you don't think that's American,
You're a radical sonofa———.

In fact, the pendulum of armed forces censorship has, in recent years, swung in the opposite direction from that in civilian life. Songs are acceptable only if bawdy or bitchy.

Perhaps this occurs because most American males are burdened with the fear that other American males will doubt their maleness. They, therefore, demonstrate their masculinity at every opportunity by constantly employing four-letter words and carefully avoiding any sign of tenderness or patriotic fervor. Most of the service songs of the last few American wars seem to bear out this surmise.

The common soldiers in the vanguard of Washington's army sang many patriotic songs. On the march they chanted:

The day is done, my boys, push on
And follow, follow Washington;
'Tis he that leads the way, my lads,
'Tis he that leads the way.

Till right prevails, our happy bands
Will fight like true Americans;
Push on, my lads, my lads, push on
And follow Washington.

Another popular favorite was the previously mentioned song written by General Joseph Warren, who perversely chose for his melody "The British Grenadiers":

Torn from a world of tyrants,
  Beneath this western sky,
We formed a new dominion,
  A land of liberty.
Then guard your rights, Americans,
  Nor stoop to lawless sway,
Huzzah, huzzah, huzzah
  For a free Amerikay.

But today there are no "Hail Pershing" or "Follow Mark Clark" songs in the balladry of the barracks. Quite the contrary.

Today it's:

The General got the Croix DeGuerre
The sonofa——— was never there.

or:

Every day we go out hiking,
Captain rides along in a big sedan;
He won't rest until he finds out
Can his car outwalk a man.

or;

We sent for the Army to come to Tulagi,
But General MacArthur said no,
And he gave as his reason,
"This isn't the season,
Besides, you got no USO."

As for such anachronistic sentiments as patriotism, the singers gave short shrift to these; and, except in one

Korean War song, managed to ignore the possibility that the enemy might have had something to do with their being in uniform. This song is such an anomaly it bears repeating:

Min Pao went way up to cold Koto-ri,
His prize Chinese army in action to see.
He thought that the battle they never could lose,
But all that he found was their hats and their shoes.

Uncle Joe Stalin, your stooges have found
It just doesn't pay to invade foreign ground,
For when they disturbed the serene morning calm,
They brought on the rockets, the bombs, and napalm.

It is true that "Rodger Young" and "Praise the Lord" were great inspirational hits during the early days of World War II, but these were written *for* the Army, not by the Army—although Frank Loesser wore his GI uniform while he was composing it in the Special Services office on 42nd Street in New York. Irving Berlin wasn't even in uniform when he wrote "The Air Corps Anthem" and "God Bless America," but they attained great popularity, especially with the Boy Scouts who have collected hundreds of thousands of dollars in royalties donated by Mr. Berlin.

Eager-beaver public relations officers turned out reams of mimeographed sheets with "fighting" songs on them, but these sheets were used for other purposes by the GI. What else could he do with such synthetics as:

Iwo Jima, here we come,
We are tough and we're not dumb;

We're steady, we're ready, we're volunteers,
We're rugged, we're salty, GI buccaneers.

Having forsworn songs of duty, love of country, or of
bravery, the American serviceman was left with the traditional material of all armies since long before Xeno-
phon. He sang of the food, "Poison, and not enough of
it," he sang of women, "of the need for a basic relationship," and he sang about the "Brass" in all its disgusting
manifestations.

Let's take some antichow examples:

They tell you in the Army, the biscuits they are fine;
One fell off the table and crushed a pal of mine.

or:

I'm sick of the food in the Philippines,
The Corregidor coffee and the Bataan beans.

Multiply these examples by hundreds and you'll begin
to realize how the men in service felt about the bakers
and cooks (usually referred to as "B. and C." with other
translations available).

For the officer class, the enlisted man's songs had especially pithy verses, such as the ones previously cited.
There are few examples of pro-officer sentiments except
in the case of the 1st Marine Raider Battalion, a very
strange outfit. One of the verses they sang is unparal-
leled in modern warfare:

We have a Colonel, his name is Sam Griffith;
In all of our battles he's right in there with us.

Certainly, Colonel Griffith was an outstanding officer, but there must have been many other brave men in the upper echelons. The songs are silent on this subject.

This 1st Marine Raider Battalion is a very special case and deserves more careful study. This is possible because there exists in private hands a wire recording, made at a New Zealand rest camp in 1943, of veterans of the devastation at Tulagi and Guadalcanal. This document is the last contact their families had with most of these men because the Division was decimated during the landings on New Georgia. Except for such throwbacks as the praise of Colonel Griffith, mentioned above, the songs of the Raiders are a perfect cross-sectional representation of service songs.

For instance, we know that each service despised all the others, and the Marines were specialists in expressing their venom:

We sent for the Coast Guard to come to Tulagi
And waited for them to appear.
They sent back a letter, "We like it here better,
But maybe we'll make it next year."
So we sent for the Navy to come to Tulagi,
The dear little Navy agreed,
In 10,000 sections—from 18 directions,
Christ, what a fouled-up stampede.
So we sent for the Air Force to come to Tulagi,
The Air Force appeared on the scenes.
They bombed out 4 donkeys, 8 horses, 3 monkeys,
And 14 platoons of Marines.

Another example of balladry from New Zealand was the rewritten ancient bawdy song "Roll Your Leg Over." Instead of such traditional verses as:

If all them young ladies were bats in the steeple
And I was a bat, there'd be more bats than people.

The Raiders sang:

Now this is the story about the 1st Raiders;
They ship us all over to fight the invaders.
We're glad all the sergeants
Are not like old Pettit;
We'd shoot the old bugger
And never regret it.
Roll your leg over, roll your leg over,
Roll your leg over the man in the moon.

Many service songs were parodies on popular tunes.
The New Zealand recordings demonstrate this fact as
well. Even beloved Colonel Griffith was in for some kid-
ding in the Marine version of an old favorite:

I want a life, just like the life
That Colonel Griffith leads;
He's got a jeep, all we've got is feet,
And boy, do we use 'em.

A famous marching song was translated into:

The M-1's bang, machine guns clang,
And the mortars blaze away;
We hope to hell we hold the line until the break of day.
There's A and B and C and D,
But no more company E,
The finest band of real Marines
That you will ever see.

For further choral fare, the Marines followed the age-
old example of American troops since the General Jo-

seph Warren episode, and borrowed from the British songbag. Thus, they sang, with faked British accents, the London Music Hall ditty:

I don't want to be a soldier,
I don't want to go to war,
I just want to run around Piccadilly underground
Living off the earnings of a high-class lady.

with the chorus:

Call out my mother, my sister, and my brother,
But for Gossakes, don't call me.

Yes, the Raiders were a singing outfit. But, right next to them in battle were many groups which sang very little except for the popular tunes that Tokyo Rose played for them daily. This phenomenon was true throughout the services. One soldier or sailor with a guitar could spark an entire regiment into chorus. The Adjutant General's office endeavored to foster a singing spirit among the troops, but their inadequate publication called *The Army Song Book* (1941) was used as a mark to hold the GI's place in his latest comic book. Group singing was a matter of chance.

In pursuit of Navy songs, I entrained for the Pentagon. The powers were very upset about the suggestion that the boys would sing anything but old sea chanteys. In an anxious desire to help my research, they handed me a neatly printed official book called *Navy Songs*. This contained such inspirational material as "The Army Goes Rolling Along" and "America The Beautiful." It actually had many fine songs in it—but enlisted men rarely learn songs from books. One guitarist in each ship's company would've been more useful.

I did find some fine songs during singing sessions with minor naval personnel. When I had a parcel of these, I decided to record them in an LP album called "Every Inch A Sailor." The night before the first session I received two phone calls. The first was from an old singmate from Boston, John C. Bull, Jr. He proceeded to sing, via long-distance, "The Laws of the Navy":

These are the laws of the Navy,
They're constant whatever they say
And they boil down to one small commandment,
The commandment says, "Thou Shalt Obey."

The other call was from Murray Phillips, another ex-Navy singer. He remembered a song from his service in Cuba:

In Guantanamo Bay, call it "Gitmo" for short,
Not much of a town, and much less of a port;
You take just one look and you know that you're seein'
The doggonedest hole in the whole Caribbean.

The Air Force was a different matter. In my book *Singing Holidays*, I pompously stated, "The Air Force is our youngest service branch. Some popular songs have been written which might do very well as theme songs, but we've decided to volunteer the following as our contribution to the songbag of the Air Force." "The following" was a mild little creation parodying the old Army song, "The Sergeant." As far as I was concerned that was as far as Air Force folksong had progressed.

On January 12, 1959, Captain William Smart, jet pilot veteran of World War II and the Korean War, sent me a privately collected and mimeographed folio of 256 traditional Air Force songs. Many of the songs had been created during World War I and refurbished in the years that followed. One of the most expressive was:

I wanted wings till I got the doggoned things,
Now I don't want them any more.
They taught me how to fly, then they sent me out to die,
I've had a bellyful of war.
Take the doggoned Zeros and give 'em to the heroes,
I'd rather have a woman than get banged up in a Grumman.
Buster,
I wanted wings till I got the doggoned things,
Now I don't want them any more.

In one case, airmen wrote a song which would have caused a civilian singer to be a subject for the attention of a lynch mob. While Stateside newspaper readers were cheered by reports of overwhelming American arms superiority, pilots were ruefully joining the chorus of "The Prettiest Ship":

(Leader) The prettiest ship
(Chorus) The prettiest ship
(Leader) Out on the line
(Chorus) Out on the line
(Leader) The MIG-15
(Chorus) The MIG-15
(Leader) Flies fast and fine

(All)   The prettiest ship out on the line
The MIG-15 flies fast and fine.

When we go up and fly at noon
The MIG-15's fly off the moon.

We chase them up to forty-four,
The fox-eight-six [F86] ain't got much more,

We're coming home with thirteen chicks,
Twelve MIG-15's, one fox-eight-six.

Korean War parodies were created by the hundreds, again antithetical to the civilian rules which proscribed ribaldry and un-American sentiment. Consider this cynical appraisal of our war aims:

I'm just a rover they hustled over
To Korea I abhor.
One for the money and two for the show,
Ridgeway said, "Stay," but we all want to go;
No use explaining why we're remaining,
We've got what they sent us for,
Korea, Korea, and diarrhea to make all the rice grow more.

The Death Rattler's Squadron, a Marine air unit in Korea, compiled a folio of well-worn songs, with the introduction: ". . . Even as we breathe in the breath, taking in the sight of a 40 mm. flak trap, these familiar strains are what make it worth while. . . ." After that poetic introduction, we are introduced to a collection of bawdy material verging on the catastrophic. In between these gems are pertinent songs of fed-up fliers:

The Midway has thousand-foot runways,
The Leyte eight hundred and ten,
But we'd not have much of a carrier,
With two of ours tied end to end.

Our catapult shots are all hairy,
Our catapult gear is red hot,
It never goes off when you're ready,
It always goes off when you're not.

These songs were created by the hundreds and sung by the men who fought on the ground, in the air, and on the sea. What happened when they returned to civilian life? Why, then, the civilian rules took effect again. Seated in an audience, surrounded by other civilians, with their wives or their dates, these barracks balladeers would themselves be horrified if their own creations were to be sung at them. Occasionally, they will accept an appropriate wartime song when it is sung in the company of former wartime buddies. When the Reserves were called up during the last Berlin crisis, this refrain was trotted out, but in laundered form:

In peacetime the regulars are happy,
In peacetime they're anxious to serve,
But just let us get into trouble,
They call out the goldarned reserves.

The censorship in the ranks of the Army and the censorship practiced by civilians are at opposite poles. The same Americans who puritanically and narrow-mindedly inhibit the singing of bawdy songs and political material sang little else themselves when uniformed for war. Is it the public platform that makes the difference? Do we reserve for small groups such lively performances? Why, then, should we not look upon a concert audience as a large collection of small groups and extend the range of our publicly performed folk music? Why should the servicemen have all the fun?

13.

The Legal Tangle

To paraphrase the Paycock, one of O'Casey's most delightful creations, the folk song world is in a state of chassis. Folk music is big business, big business means big money, and big money is the compost pile which encourages the growth of the seven deadly sins. The possibility of provoking excessive wealth has caused sober and honest men to assault the bastion of the public domain.

America's copyright laws allow a writer or composer to keep title to his composition for twenty-eight years from the date of first publication. At the end of twenty-eight years, he is allowed to renew his registration for another twenty-eight years. After that period—fifty-six years of personal ownership—the property becomes the property of all, or more precisely, the property of none. Every year hundreds of songs become the playthings of the populace, free of royalty charges or licensing fees.

These maturing musical properties are as nothing compared with the tremendous reservoir of traditional song. According to the law, folk music is also in the public domain. Yet practice has almost dissolved the theory of the law. But every day old folk songs are being registered for new copyrights. Every day some folk singer, or collector, or publisher sues some other folk singer, collector, or publisher for using some folk song without paying tribute or a fee.

What would happen in the book publishing field if any publisher had the right to publish on his own—if he paid a slight royalty—any book published by a rival company? Well, in the music business, any recording company can record any song previously recorded, if it pays the publisher the statutory royalty of two cents per record.

Let us follow the adventures of a fictitious song through the traditional process until it becomes the first of the top ten. For two centuries (let us say), the Cratchit family sang the songs their forefather, Devil Bob, brought with him to America from Fraserburgh in Aberdeenshire. Young Tim Cratchit, called "Tiny" because he is six foot six, loved best the old ballad "Sir Dougald in the Kirk":

"Where hae ye been, Sir Dougald?
Where hae ye been all day?"

"I hae been to the kirk sin morning,
And yet was nae able to pray.

"Ken ye the dochter of Morah,
She that is passing fair?
She sang the song of the seventh son,
And, ach, I heard naething mair."

Once upon a time, a nearsighted city man drove by in a dusty car and heard Tiny Tim's favorite ballad. He stopped his car, unpacked an Ampex 350 recording machine and a Telefunken microphone, complete with battery-powered condenser. With this primitive equipment, he proceeded to record Tim's singing of his favorite song, then packed his gear and drove off.

The nearsighted city man, without his horn-rimmed glasses, was a fairly personable individual. Lecturing to his Medieval Literature classes, he sang his new acquisition and was surprised at the excited approbation. Looking at his profile in a three-way mirror, he decided to sing his song on a local television educational channel. After this venture, which was a huge success, he published, through the local University press, a collection of the songs he had found on his journey.

Some of his students learned the song and took it with them when they went home for the Easter holidays. Two of the undergraduates, who were proficient on the bongo and Brownie bass, performed the ballad and its three hundred and twenty verses at a coffee house. The star of the coffee house show asked them to teach him the song so that he could sing it on his next record album. With great pride the two undergraduates taught the star their precious song and were rewarded with a free cup of coffee.

This tangled web I am spinning is not a wild fantasy. It is very close to the true adventures of many modern songs. To continue, the song was well received as recorded. But it did not receive an important reception until Ronnie Hayman, a well-known folk song rewriter, recast it in modern terms:

"Where have you been, oh, honey?
Where have you been today?"
"Standing behind you, baby,
But I didn't have nothing to say."

Realizing that he had a valuable property, Ronnie hurried over to the manager of the Sisters Eleven—a folk singing group which had once been a female football team—and sang the new lyrics. The Sisters recorded the number as the "A" side of their latest release, and it made number thirty on the charts in its first week, number ten the second week, and number two the third week.

The song was credited "Words and Music by Ronnie Hayman." At once, the coffee house star sued Ronnie's publishing firm, the two undergraduates sued Ronnie's publishing firm, the collector sued Ronnie's publishing firm, and Tiny Tim Cratchit scratched his head and declared that he couldn't sing his favorite song anymore because it had been "spiled rotten." There are two questions to be asked before we bring our epic story to a conclusion. First, who deserved the royalties derived from the song? Secondly, who got them?

There are many good people who believe that "Sir Dougald" was no one's special property and that no royalties should have been paid to anyone. The backwoods people agreed that Tiny Tim Cratchit really owned the song by hereditary right. The publishing world agreed that the song wouldn't have got anywhere without the expert work of Ronnie Hayman. Our personable Medieval Literature professor and his students were enraged that they were not profiting from their scholarship.

Most folk song authorities believe that the revenues from any song should be given to the collector of the original song. But the law threw the professor's claim out of court. He had himself written that the songs were public domain—uncopyrightable. And the coffee house star was, at the moment of recording, merely repeating a song in the public domain. Besides, the copyright law affirms that a work published without copyright protection falls into the public domain. And recent cases imply that the distribution of a phonograph record is a publication.

One recent case concerns the song "The Cotton Fields Away." Leadbelly and his wife, Martha, spent some time with the eminent collector and writer, Fred Ramsay. During their sojourn, they sang and talked for hours into a microphone which relayed their conversation and music into the waiting tape recorder. After Leadbelly's death, Ramsay decided that the material was too important to keep to himself and allowed Moe Asch to release the edited conversations as "Leadbelly's Last Sessions." Among the songs was "The Cotton

Fields Away." Years went by and the song was recorded by many important performers, all of whom concluded that it was public domain material. Then Leadbelly's publisher, Howard Richmond, sued for court
recognition of Leadbelly's common-law copyright. His
contention? Leadbelly had given no one permission to
release the song as a record. It is possible that the copyright might be returned to the Leadbelly estate.

There is another problem. Each singer makes changes
in the song as he sings it. Often this is done inadvert-
ently and many singers have been shocked when an
early recording of a favorite song was played for them.
The collector, too, often makes changes in order to get
the material accepted by the publisher, or to fit a long
song into a short chapter. The Lomaxes, John A. and
Alan after him, often chose their favorite verses and
melodies from among many versions and submitted
these for printing. Wasn't this an act of creative selection? Many folklorists did sizable rewrite jobs on the
material. The most painstaking, like Cecil Sharp, indicated where these alterations had been made. Many
others hid their handiwork under the proverbial bushel.

Even if his common-law copyright doesn't apply,
Tiny Cratchit should be compensated if his contributions are adopted as part of the popular recording.
The near-sighted collector may have made some
changes, too. If his changes are used, he should be compensated—even though he foolishly permitted a recording without claiming ownership. If the coffee-shop boys
made changes, and these were used, they deserve part
of the spoils. And then there's folk song rewriter Ronnie

Hayman. He deserves a part of the pot. In fact, he is the only one who would derive any revenues from the song because the hit record was a substantial change from the original ballad.

But let's make the situation more tortuous—and, consequently, more true to life. Suppose the hit record were a version of the collected version, which was a version of the original sung version? Suppose the song were "Tom Dooley"? Frank Proffitt, a real person, sang "Tom Dooley," a song about a real person, to Frank Warner, also a real person. Warner recorded the song for Elektra Records without copyrighting it, and Alan Lomax reproduced it in his book *Folk Song, U. S. A.* with Frank's permission. Many folk singers repeated the song, some even crediting Warner as the collector. One day The Kingston Trio heard it, enjoyed it, learned it, and recorded it—almost exactly as Frank Warner had recorded it.

By law, The Kingston Trio could copyright their musical arrangement. They asked for the royalties and the record company granted the request. It was, after all, their own arrangement they were using. Moreover, they were *The* Kingston Trio, and the company was happy to pay them the two cents for each record sold. In the case of a hit song, the record companies seek to be protected from infringement suits. Consequently, they will often sign a licensing agreement with any writer who has a claim to the song and will sign a contract taking upon himself all financial and legal responsibility.

Of course, they try to ensure that the "composer"

credited really has some proprietary right to the property since the first step of a counterclaimant is to enjoin
all royalty payments—a very messy business. In some
cases, a large recording company will seek out a composer to protect themselves when a song's origin is in
question. It is for that reason that my name is listed as
composer of "Old King Cole" on Harry Belafonte's
"Carnegie Hall #2" LP. Actually, it was old when London Bridge was still a plank and "Beowulf" was the
Book of the Month.

The Record company was happy to credit the Trio
for "Tom Dooley," but Lomax objected. He had copyrighted the song before the Trio had recorded it. Ah,
responded the Trio, but that was after Warner had
propelled the song into the public domain by recording
it without copyrighting it. Besides, what right had
Warner to the song when he admitted he was singing it
exactly as he'd learned it from Proffitt? Warner, a hearty,
friendly man, didn't really feel like fighting the case
until someone played a recording of his singing "Tom
Dooley" years before. Then he realized that he had
changed the song, and that his changes had possibly
helped the record become popular. The tangle is in for
a long untangling—and the courts will not easily re-
solve the problem.

Today the licensing agencies and the publishers are
busy working out tortuous scales of compensation
where use of public domain material is concerned. But
the courts are busy handing down opinions which serve
to bemuse the interested parties. These are based on
the court's attempts to serve justice. But new develop-

ments in the music and recording industry make this hard. For instance, take the case of the Russian *Etude*. In 1956, the Federal Circuit Court of Appeal sitting in Chicago awarded a copyright to a composer who admitted that "the melodic element of this *Etude* is from a Russian folk song." Another composer took this melody and wrote new words to it. Ordinarily, one would expect that the second composer had the right to copyright his "new song." But the court, to give the original copyrighter protection against being copied, held that, in the case of this obscure, not easily obtainable song, he had made enough of an original contribution when he put it down on paper as he remembered it.

It's easy to understand why the radio and television authorities have become jittery where folk music is concerned. If I were to sing "The Battle Hymn of the Republic" on a program, the "music clearance" department would insist on knowing the name of some book or publisher who would be willing to claim authorship. In some cases folk singers, unable to find their favored songs in available collections, have ascribed them to companies willing to accept the responsibility. This compounds the problem, by producing many copyrights to some folk songs—complicating the courts' search for the proper owner.

In 1948 I composed the song, "When I First Came to This Land." I sang it at a Town Hall program. I included it in my book *Singing Holidays*. Thereafter, a West Coast writer refurbished it and brought it to the attention of the popular group, The Limeliters. Their recording of the song was very well received, but not by me—for the song was ascribed to the West Coast writer. When I objected, I was told that a substantial change had been made and that I was, therefore, stripped of my rights. Fortunately, I had never recorded the song before my book appeared, and so I was reinstated as the author. But, it is with a sickening recollection that I observe the 25 LP's on my shelf, complete with many original songs, and many rewritten traditional songs, which I recorded before I was aware of the legal implications.

In an article in *Sing Out,* Irwin Silber ruefully points out that Jesse Cavanaugh and Arnold Stanton claimed authorship of "The Roving Kind," although their copyright was dated two years after the song had been printed in his publication. This recalls another incident. A young lady named Midge Brodie taught me the song in 1940 as "The Rakish Kind":

My daddy is a minister, a good and righteous man,
My mother is a Methodist,
I do the best I can . . .

I enjoyed singing the rakish words and shared my enjoyment with an audience in Boston, on a program with Leadbelly and a pretty young female singer. The pretty young female asked me to teach her the song, and, naturally, I complied. Her next move was to record the song and bill herself as "One of the Rakish Kind." This was entirely proper, especially since, on occasion, she would tell the audience that she had learned the song from me—just as I explained that Midge Brodie had taught it to me.

The song became popular in folksinging circles. A few years later, when The Weavers recorded the song for Decca, they decided to protect themselves from previous claims by rewriting some of the words and calling it "The Roving Kind." The pretty young female singer could hardly be restrained from suing to protect her rights. People's Songs deplored the copyrighting of a traditional song, however altered, especially since they had printed the original. Midge Brodie never complained, nor did the original composer, dead these two hundred years.

But responsible folk song authorities are complaining. They feel that scholarship has suffered as a result of this unwholesome legal situation. They point to the recent publication of a collection of folk songs by one of our most respected collectors. Every one of the songs has been carefully changed, melodically and lyrically, in order to support the claim of the editor, "with new music and new words." American collectors are making substantial changes in their songs in order to win recognition should their "properties" turn out to be located at the foot of the recording rainbow.

J. Frank Dobie, the great Texas writer and folklorist, declared, "I didn't make up these songs. I can't claim them as my property. Anyone who wants to use them is welcome. Anyone who wants to make money out of them can do that, too, if he can square his conscience." But the austere International Folk Music Council has stated that the collector who made the first written copy of the song should be accorded the copyright, as if his notation were an original composition. This would, it appears, exclude any possibility that the singer of the songs might be considered as having some rights in the matter.

I will not try to absolve myself from some assignment of guilt. Having lost title to many original productions and to many rewritten songs, I have begun to inscribe on the title pages of most of the items in my repertory the legend, "New words and new music by Oscar Brand." When one of our leading popular groups asked me to program for them an album of traditional songs, I found myself making "substantial changes" in the material. At one point, the record company was so carried away with its desire to please me that they ascribed to me the authorship of "The Battle Hymn of the Republic."

At this point, the reader must be cognizant of a wild confusion existing in laws covering folk music. Let us further becloud the issues. During the depression of the '30's, the government, among its "boondoggles," established agencies to collect and publicize American traditional music. Much of this material entered the archives of American Folk Song deposited in the Library of Congress. The Library itself hired collectors to bring in recordings of folk songs. Many of these collectors published the results in books, without the permission of their sources. This led to further claims and counterclaims.

In England, veteran singer and collector A. L. Lloyd has been lobbying for "a proper and just law . . . concerning the ownership and use of material." Lloyd, however, warns that legal codification may result in publishers' refusing singers the right to sing the songs. He offers no solution, but hopes that the collector receives some reward for having "gone to the trouble and expense to secure a version of a piece of folk music such as may enrich the lives of many thousands of people."

The American Folklore Society has appointed a Committee on Copyrights to investigate and produce some suggested plan. Perhaps they would do well to examine the suggestion of Irwin Silber, editor of *Sing Out*. Silber proposes a ". . . Folk Song Foundation which can function much as BMI does in the popular song field— collecting royalties on traditional song and using the money for grants in folk song scholarship, for publication (in book and record form) of the folk song treasures stored in the Library of Congress, and for some payment to the original singers and collectors who have helped to keep alive this important part of our national heritage."

Let us begin with this proposition and extend it somewhat. Should a composer or writer make changes in a folk song, he would be entitled to a percentage of the royalties accruing to the song. The percentage should be decided by a committee on the basis of the extent of the rewriter's contribution. The remainder of the money would be placed in the Foundation to endow studies in folk song and finance further collecting.

Choosing this committee would be a very difficult task. Very few reputable authorities have been able to keep themselves out of the arena of public involvement.

Lomax, Sandburg, Emrich, Cazden, and many others are personally involved in the problem. But there are authorities left who could take on the formidable job.

In Berkeley there is Bertrand Bronson, in New Mexico Oliver LaFarge. Ben Botkin, Rae Korson, and Harry Oster are not only expert, but enlightened and incorruptible. Charles Seeger, George Korson, J. Frank Dobie, and Edgar Stanley Hyman could adjudicate any copyright dispute. And such delightful people as New Englanders Evelyn Wells, Helen Flanders, and Una Ritchie Yahkub would make for a handsome-looking council.

There is in Italy a law which performs a similar function. Where public domain material is used, part of the proceeds from exploitation of the resulting song is paid into a fund for aged and indigent musicians. Theodora Zavin, who with Harriet Pilpel wrote the lucid handbook of law, *Rights and Writers,* believes that this would never work in America. "With only seven notes to work with, it is likely that any composer could be accused of having public domain material in his compositions." However, we believe that a jury such as we've suggested could be trusted to avoid such inequities.

In conclusion, let me once again point out the confused state of the legal approach to folk music. The laws are producing a situation in which one group copyrights a song and another group records the same song and then copyrights it for themselves. Then the record companies pay each group the required two cents royalty fee. The status quo often deprives the original singer of any recompense, and usually ignores the claim of the original collector. Most of the people who today profit from folk songs despised the vulgar effusions of the common people until the bandwagon came past their disordered front porches. Up to now each singer, collector, or popularizer has had to shift for himself, resorting to subterfuge or legal trickery to obtain some part of the rewards. This is not a very healthy manifestation and has caused great concern in the folk song community.

There is now under way an extensive Congressional examination of the copyright law—under the direction of the Library of Congress. The revisions will certainly clarify the meaning of the term publication, where phonograph records are concerned. And the problems of the folk music world will certainly be re-examined in order to achieve more equitable solutions. There is hope.

14.

The Clouded Future

To forecast the future of folk music is a very easy task. By the time the future comes along, the forecast will be forgotten by the reader. If it is wrong, no one will remember. If it is correct, the author will see to it that everyone is reminded. It is on this principle that most of our newspaper columnists derive their reputation for fortunetelling. I have made many predictions in my time. For instance, I am the fellow who refused to copyright seven rewritten *Bawdy Songs* L.P.'s because "nobody would want to use them." Since then six of these have been adapted by now wealthy writers. And there was the time a friend of mine invited me to the preview of a cowboy picture and asked if I thought the title song might become popular. I explained patiently and firmly that "High Noon" was a very nice song, but hadn't a chance in the popular market.

When Elvis Presley led the parade for rock 'n' roll, I commented that he was very good, but that rock 'n' roll was a passing fancy. In 1962, I revised my opinion and predicted that the new form would be with us for a long time. Immediately after this, three stations switched to sweet swing. However, I must remind the reader that these errors were the result of ignorance and confusion, and were not made for venal or self-seeking reasons.

For instance, I believe that the present popularity of folk-song forms will continue and that, in fact, the vogue will increase. It is only fair to point out though that many observers do not share this opinion. Columnists, jazz buffs, and opera fans are predicting with even, sure tones that the folk music fad will soon be over. This may be merely wishful thinking. Many of these prophets of doom are motivated by the fear of excessive penetration into the domain of their own beloved predilections.

For instance, the columns of *The Village Voice*, a remarkably interesting Greenwich Village weekly, were enlivened recently by an excessive attack upon folk music by a dissident named Robert Reisner. In his article, "The Menace of Folk Music," this angry young man declared, "The humble, monotonous, skimmed-milk folk song is pushing classical and jazz albums out of homes." He went on to describe the male folk fan as a dirty, unkempt, sandal-shod neurotic. The female of the species, he described as dressed in the uniform of beatism—black leotards, long, straight, dank hair, and an ugly oversized sweater.

The following week, *Times* critic Robert Shelton, one of our most incisive commentators on the subject of contemporary trends in traditional song, responded with a scornful typewriter: "Some of Reisner's half-cooked canards deserve a roasting." Where Reisner wrote, "There are no standards of wit or intelligence," Shelton responded, "He is obviously unaware of the songs of Woody Guthrie, Ernie Marrs, or Malvina Reynolds." Where Reisner pointed his accusing finger at the prevailing folk song costume, "All you need are some dirty clothes," Shelton retorted, "Some of Reisner's folknik neighbors—the Clancy Brothers, Molly Scott, Logan English, Jack Keenan, Ray Boguslav—are neat, attractive people."

Reisner concluded, "When Bikel, Belafonte, and Brand replace Bach, Beethoven, and Brahms, it's a bad scene." It doesn't seem necessary to point out that Bikel, Belafonte, and Brand would agree with this thesis. Luckily, it will probably never come to pass. Most folk music lovers manage to find room in their affections, and on their record shelves, for Bach, Beethoven, Brahms, Bikel, and John Coltrane.

On the whole, this is probably just a pleasant game the boys are playing. They all believe that folk music will persist despite its own narrow-minded adherents and the fears of other cultists. The man of the near future will probably broaden his horizons, not limit them. The pop snobs, the classic snobs, and the folk snobs may all rest easy. My first major prediction for the future is that there will be enough room in the Elysian fields for the pastorale and the pastoral. Co-existence is the watchword for the coming decades.

What will the folk music of the forthcoming years be like? The most pessimistic outlook is that of A. L. Lloyd, the thoughtful British singer-writer, in his excellent pamphlet, "The Singing Englishman." Lloyd speaks sadly of the end of industrial folk songs—"In general, the coming of industrialization and the substitution of machine labour for hand labour meant that the songs died away very quickly." As examples, he gives the sea chanties and the songs of the sickle reaper.

Wiss a raw a rue a raw,
Wiss a raw a rue a ray.

"When the sickle reaper disappeared, not only did the songs that went with his arm go, but other popular songs died at the same time which pictured the reaper's image and described his work."

He doesn't give up hope for folk songs, but he does declare that it is useless to try to revive music that has nothing to do with contemporary social life. "It may be that we shall have to wait till society is so altered that there is no longer any special distinction or variance between the composer and the rest of his fellowmen." His approach implies that there will be no true folk music again until serious music and popular music have become one. This belief is, I think, the new dialectic. It seems to ignore a tremendous body of modern folk song as pertinent as "The Talking Atomic Blues" of Vern

Partlow, and even Woody Guthrie's "Jesus Christ," to the tune of "Jesse James."

More important, this Lloydian analysis would seem to deny the popularity of "Sixteen Tons" or "The Battle of New Orleans." And how could it be possible that millions of city-bred young men and women would be singing "The Boll Weevil" without ever having seen cotton, except in the form of bobby socks and chino pants. Once again it is necessary to recall Ed Mc-Curdy's rueful, "I have never been a motherless child, but I know what it is to be sad."

For more optimistic estimations, with which I am in full accord, we should turn to the homilies of Mrs. Emma Dusenberry, one of America's great traditional singers. Collector Sam Eskin reported that Mrs. Dusenberry observed, "I set out to learn all the songs in the world. But after a while I had to give up because people kept on making up new ones." Sam followed this statement with one of his own, "The sounds of our times get into the singing of these songs and make them interesting to today's listeners who might find the style of the old times strange."

In *Caravan*, another respected singer and collector, Sam Hinton, pointed out that our contemporary balladeers—especially the urban variety—"are singing the songs for the songs' own sake." In other words, many of our old ballads are being performed and enjoyed without change in their archaic forms because they seem to have some validity for the modern age. It is true that some of the references in old songs may be obscure to modern listeners, and some of the words may be obsolete, but the audience seems to be able to bridge the centuries-old gap. Sometimes when I sing "The Good-for-Nothing Boys," I interpolate an explanation for the first verse:

Come along, girls, and listen to my noise,
Don't go marrying those good-for-nothing boys,
If you do your fortune it will be,
Hoe-cake, hominy, and sassafras tea.
(That's as bad as C-rations.)

However, I've discovered that often the audience gets the significance of the song without any help from modern terminology. The song itself has a form which fights against misunderstanding even after one hundred years have passed.

It is my belief that many of our folk songs will be sung to happy audiences in the future with little "popularizing." A workman or an executive who hates the boss needs no translation to enjoy "Johnny Come Down to Hilo":

The first mate he was pretty bad,
But the Captain was the Devil's Dad.

And every young man with a maid will chuckle at this succinct verse in the same song:

I tied my girl in a "tater sack,"
She'll be true to me till I get back.

To conclude my first prediction: folk songs will become more and more popular without being updated or popularized. By the time this prediction is read, I would not be surprised if some ancient ballad had found its way to the top of the popular song list.

Our second expectation of future benefits is suggested by Mrs. Dusenberry's remarks. With modifications suggested by modern needs, old folk songs will reach new heights of popularity. It is this expected manifestation, however, which will provoke the most controversy among folk song fans. In order to clarify the issues, we shall arbitrarily call one side "purist" and the other "popularizer."

The purist draws his cohorts from among the historians, the ethnic fanatics or "fanethnics," and the thousands who have been offended by the bad taste displayed by some of the popularizers. Each of these factions has a well-footed stand, but, in some areas, their ground is clay-filled. The popularizer has many faces, some of them pleasant, others hideous. He may be a genuinely devoted lover of traditional song anxious to share his adoration with the rest of the world. Or he may be a greedy man willing to alter, subvert, emasculate, even deprecate the material if this will bring him money or power.

The purists are afraid that the greedy men will ruin the good name of folk music. They are afraid that bad songs will drive out good songs. They are afraid that the mass audience will get to hear folk-type music only in the chromium-bedecked presentations of the popularizers. One of the leaders of this faction is the peppery *Little Sandy Review*. In most of its issues, it joins battle with "Kingston Trio-type folkum," and worries that this will replace real folk music. This thesis bears examination and appraisal.

The historians and scholars, in many cases, join hands with the purists in order to protect the hunting grounds. If they are to catalogue the expressions of the past, they must have some assurance that they are not dealing with remakes. Unlike the art scholar who must validate an ancient painting, they have no easy criteria—age of canvas, types of pigments, individualism in brush strokes. In part, they must listen with heightened sensitivity for the truth of the statement and measure it against what they know of the period to which the lyric is attributed. It is a difficult task.

One night, at Carnegie Hall, I sang a version of "The Great Silkie of Sule Skerry." One of the experts in the audience whispered to his companion, "Now that's the real thing—not like some of the other songs that have been sung on this program." At the end of the song I announced that the melody had been recently written, by a young man named Waters, in the ancient modal style. The expert was embarrassed and unhappy. But he needn't have been. What he was really saying was, "That song is right—it has the earmark of tradition." And, as I have tried to indicate since the beginning of this volume, the sound is what counts, in my estimation.

But the scholar must concern himself with chronology and cataloguing. And so he deplores the liberties taken with the old songs. Since, for the most part, it is the scholar who provides the popularizer with the grist for his remunerative mill, we can sympathize with the injured feelings of a man who labors while others glean the profit. But, as the popularizer brings more and more people to the folk song fold, more old broadsides and songbooks are discovered which shed light on the attitudes and expressions of people who lived in the long ago. How wonderfully pertinent to listen to a Civil War song, as sung during that frightful conflagration, while looking at a *Harper's* illustration of the incident that provoked the song. This is the stuff by which verity is assured. Wherever possible, it must be safeguarded.

However, the popularizers cannot be prevented from perusing the scholarly collections to assess their popularity index. Will this song be another "Tom Dooley"? Will this clapping song be the successor to "The Cotton Fields Away"? If there is something compelling in the tune or lyric, this will certainly be seized upon and refurbished for the common market. And millions may share in the enjoyment of the song. Although purists will say this is a dreadful consummation, they have yet to prove that this development destroys the original song. This final question is the important one—can a refurbished copy destroy an original? To answer "Yes" shows little faith in the strength of the unchanged folk song.

Some of the purists agree that the original song will persist, but object to some of the popularizers for reasons bearing upon their own conceptions of good and bad taste. For instance, Ron Radosh, in *Sing Out*, agrees that "commercialism in itself is not an evil . . ." Then he points to the success of The Weavers in the early days when "they combined an understanding of the music with good arrangements, sound musical taste, and down-to-earth personality and feeling in their presentations." However, Radosh deplores The Weavers' later attempt to alter their material—"To gain a successful commercial comeback in 1958, The Weavers thought they had to resort to ruining good songs. One such attempt was a rock 'n' roll parody of 'Take This Hammer,' called 'Take This Letter and Carry It to My Darling!' The record included a ripping sound for the opening of the letter."

In my opinion, this anger against popularization is a salutary manifestation. It will continue in the future, as will the commercialism. And when the popularizer steps outside the bounds of good taste and decency, the sounds of fury may help force him back. Certainly no one objected to The Weavers' rewrite which created "Kisses Sweeter Than Wine." And no one objected when Woodrow Wilson Guthrie took the old frontier ballad about Billy the Kid and substituted his own lyrics to create an inspiring anthem to America—"Pastures of Plenty."

Unfortunately, this type of tasteful change has not been predominant. The Kingston Trio—which has performed many songs with musical skill and verve—have stooped to degrading parodies of Spanish-speaking Americans with their "Mañana" approach to "Coplas." The Limeliters, whose potential is tremendous, make a homosexual travesty of "The Cumberland Mountain Bear Chase." This last exciting banjo piece has also suffered somewhat in Peter Seeger's children's version, but few purists will quarrel with Seeger. Just a few days before writing this chapter, I watched a new "folk group" perform at a large night club. They were really crowd pleasers, and the audience laughed at many of the sallies. For instance, Woody Guthrie's children's song, "Car Car" was described as "the worst song submitted so far," and the implication was that it was an immature grownups' song. A few seconds later, the tender, stirring "Old Blue" was described as a children's song. It is this sort of irresponsibility which makes not only purists angry, but enrages any person of sensibility. Nevertheless, it is to be hoped in the future that these lapses from good taste will diminish. After all, most popular folk artists have good taste—otherwise they wouldn't have chosen folk music in the first place.

Folk music as "special material" will be even more prevalent in the future. Many of the leading vocal artists in the country are including folk songs in their repertory. The purist would comment bitterly that the over-arranged folk song might as well be a Schubert Lied. But this will not stop the trend. Concert artists will continue programing any folk song that suits their fancy. And performers who sing folk songs will feel free to revise and rearrange them to fulfill their own needs.

Once in a while, the concert artists and popularizers will even object to the ethnic-centered folk song lover as a detriment to the art. William Clauson, one of America's hardest-working minstrels, is one of the many concert artists who turned to folk music for the material with which to woo his international audience. Clauson could qualify as leader of the popularizer faction with his recent statement, "A group of ultra-ultra purists—bearded and not too well washed—are taking over folk singing. They talk a lot about authentic presentation of the songs, which seems to mean copying the style of an older generation of singers such as Huddie Ledbetter."

Here we find the popularizer speaking as if the purist were an interloper. And, in a way, the purist deserves the opprobrium, since many of his favorite singers are trained musicians who took to folk music late in life. As we mentioned earlier, these include Leon Bibb, Odetta, Joan Baez, Ed McCurdy, and many others. Actually, it is our belief that, in the future, purist and popularizer will play important roles. The purist will go to the more simple singers, study the recordings of the old experts, and try to copy their songs and styles. The popularizer will change the material, perform it on a mass scale, and proselytize thousands who would not have listened to the original.

If the past is any clue, the future will then bring us a continuation of a remarkable phenomenon. For an incisive description of what we may call "ethnophilia," we turn again to the reporter from *Mademoiselle* quoted in earlier chapters: "When a student learns nowadays that folk music makes him 'feel good,' his behavior often falls into a certain pattern." The article describes the path of the ethnophile from Harry Belafonte and The Kingston Trio to the coffee houses and less popular singers. He may then progress to an appreciation of Library of Congress field recordings. Then he gets hold of a guitar or banjo and spends hours each day practicing. He plays the LP's of his favorite folk

singer in order to compare his own instrumentation
with that of the master. He begins to frequent book
stores and folklore centers searching for broadsides and
old collections. He subscribes to folk music magazines
and begins arguing with other ethnophiles about obscure passages in little-known ballads.

It is at this point that the newly formed fanatic turns
with rending fury upon his progenitors. He begins to
hate Belafonte, The Kingston Trio, and all the performers whose work brought him into the fold. In the future,
more and more of these neophytes will turn against the
artists that first set them on the road to "purity." Furthermore, many of the young singers cannot forgive fate
for having started them off in urban environments.
They want to *be* sharecroppers, they want to *be* dirt
farmers, they want to *be* blind Negro street singers.
Since this is denied them, their rage is boundless, and it
is turned upon anyone who reminds them of their own
roots in modern life. The results of this mass revulsion
will probably produce a more ethnic-centered popular
music.

In the field of jazz, there will be even more attention
paid to folk themes. And in the province of serious composition, the emphasis will continue to be laid upon
native airs for inspiration and melodic stimulation.
More and more "traditional suites" and "folk song arrangements" will enrich the concert stage. There will
probably be an important breakthrough in the operatic
field. Since "Porgy and Bess," "Sing Out Sweet Land,"
"Ballet Ballads," and "Down in the Valley," there has
been no folk opera. Soon, perhaps, we'll hear some tra-

ditional singspiels as vital as "The Beggar's Opera." The
audience is waiting.

In the past, many of our most creative choreogra-
phers, including Agnes De Mille, Hanya Holm, Donald
McKayle, and others, have used folk themes and patterns for inspiration. In the future, this practice should
become even more widespread and even more acceptable.

The popular dance will probably favor more ethnic
forms too. After all, "the twist" is a development of
Afro-Latin choreography set to a simple "eight-to-the-
bar" accompaniment. This "Black Continent" deriva-
tion gave us blues, boogie-woogie, and rock 'n' roll—all
developments of Negro folk music. What will come
next? At the time of this writing, the twist is on the
way out and many of our leading stations have banned
rock 'n' roll. It must be noted that the ban is predicated
on the "loss of audience" principle, not on any high
moral plane. Audiences will get weary of any mass-
produced art.

It is possible that the next new craze will center
around the foreign folk song. For instance, some of the
new Eurasian music, the result of Western influences on
Oriental cultures, may become popular. I've heard some
Japanese and Chinese songs which have a truly fascinating sound. Our own modal scales and Indian music
have prepared us for this eventuality, and some of our
recent Israeli importations have been pentatonic. Combined with the music which will soon be pouring out of
the aggressive little African nations, this will certainly
provide our Hit Parade with plenty of grist.

Meanwhile, our traditional songs will keep in step with the parade of the Top Ten. Country music, which has been a hardy perennial, may diminish in influence insofar as the northern urban centers are concerned. The reason for this belief is that country music is becoming almost as banal and remote from reality as were the neo-plastic creations of Tin Pan Alley. The audience will soon demand material which reflects more accurately the present day human condition.

Here lies one of the most exciting areas in which folk music will be exploited. There will be hundreds of "Talking Galaxy Blues," cosmic parodies of "On Top of Old Smoky," new space-travel versions of "Casey Jones," and even cold war rewrites of "Abdul The BulBul Amir." Many of these will find their way to the popular song lists as more and more Americans concern themselves with current events. It is certain, therefore, that radio and television programs will start to feature these musical observations. At the moment, an anti-war song by Peter Seeger, "Where Have All The Flowers Gone?", is being sung into popularity by some of our best-known folk groups.

There are indications daily in our newspapers of the future tidal currents in folk music and popular song. The son of our first spaceman is revealed to be a folk singer. The head of the Peace Corps is an admitted guitarist, and fans of traditional music now occupy the White House. These harbingers lead us to expect greater things in the highly sensitive mass media. We can expect more government sponsorship of folk music in the future.

A leader in this movement is the Department of Health, Education and Welfare. Recently, the Secretary was interrogated by a House appropriations subcommittee concerning "The World of Folk Music," which had as its first master of ceremonies Burl Ives, and after the first thirteen weeks Oscar Brand. Mr. Ribicoff revealed in a memorandum that the program carries social security information, and is currently being subscribed to by 1,300 radio stations. Few of the other government-sponsored public service programs have had such enthusiastic acceptance. It is certain that the other agencies will be reminded of this success when the time comes to program their own new shows.

As folk music becomes more and more respectable, some of the more important figures in the field may yet become national heroes. The future will bring us a motion picture treatment of "The Adventures of a Ballad Hunter," possibly titled, "The John A. Lomax Story" or "Home On The Range." It's very likely that Woody Guthrie's "Bound For Glory" will beat out Burl Ives' life story as the first Broadway musical about a folk singer. For, though "Finian's Rainbow" featured a guitar-playing hero named "Woody," folk-fan Yip Harburg generally ignored real folk material in his lyrics.

Perhaps the government will send folk singers abroad as ambassadors of good will. A national recreation association has already exposed Cisco Huston, Tony Saletan, and others to foreign audiences. Soon, I expect, the State Department will sponsor our participation in Eisteddfods, festivals, and other international meetings. Up to now, Americans who have contested African, European, and Asiatic superiority in the folk music field have had to pay their own entry fees and transportation.

In general, I expect to see more traditional song in every part of American life. I expect to hear complaints and bitter debates on the "bastardization" of our national music. But I believe we shall all benefit as a result of this large-scale infiltration—purist, popularizer, and neutral alike. The Ballad Mongers have done very little harm in reacting to a stimulus which has excited all America.

Selected Bibliography

Botkin, Benjamin A. (ed.). *A Treasury of American Folklore*. New York: Crown Publishers, 1944.

Bronson, Bertrand H. *The Traditional Tunes of the Child Ballads*. Princeton: Princeton University Press, 1959.

Dearmer, Percy, and others. *Oxford Book of Carols*. New York: Oxford University Press, Inc., 1928.

Dichter, Harry (ed.). *Handbook of American Sheet Music*. Philadelphia: Albert Saifer.

Doerflinger, William Main. *Shantymen and Shanty Boys*. New York: The Macmillan Co., 1951.

Dolph, Edward Arthur. *Sound Off*. New York: Farrar & Rinehart, Inc., 1929.

Dorson, Richard M. *American Folklore*. Chicago: University of Chicago Press, 1959.

Fowke, Edith, and Joe Glazer. *Songs of Work and Freedom*. Garden City: Doubleday & Company, Inc., 1960.

Greenway, John. *American Folk Songs of Protest*. Philadelphia: University of Pennsylvania Press, 1953.

Guthrie, Woody. *Bound for Glory*. New York: Doubleday & Company, Inc., 1943.

Korson, George (ed.). *Pennsylvania Songs and Legends*. Baltimore: The Johns Hopkins Press.

Lawless, Ray M. *Folksingers and Folksongs in America*. New York: Duell, Sloan & Pearce, Inc., 1960.

Leach, MacEdward, and Tristam P. Coffin (eds.). *The Critics and The Ballad*. Carbondale: Southern Illinois University Press, 1960.

Leach, Maria (ed.). *Standard Dictionary of Folklore, Mythology and Legend*. New York: Funk and Wagnalls Company, 1950.

Lomax, Alan. *Folk Songs of North America.* Garden City: Doubleday & Company, Inc., 1960.

Lomax, John A. *Cowboy Songs, and Other Frontier Ballads.* New York: The Macmillan Co., 1910.

McDaniel, William R., and Harold Seligman. *Grand Ole Opry.* New York: Greenberg, Publisher, 1956.

Neeser, Robert W. *American Naval Songs and Ballads.* New Haven: Yale University Press, 1938.

Opie, Iona, and Peter Opie (eds.). *Oxford Dictionary of Nursery Rhymes.* New York: Oxford University Press, 1951.

Read, Oliver, and Walter L. Welch. *From Tin Foil to Stereo.* Indianapolis: The Bobbs-Merrill Company, Inc., 1959.

Reeves, James (ed.). *The Idiom of the People: English Traditional Verse from Mss. of Cecil J. Sharp.* New York: The Macmillan Co., 1958.

Ritchie, Jean. *Singing Family of the Cumberlands.* New York: Oxford University Press, 1955.

Seeger, Ruth Crawford. *American Folk Songs for Children.* New York: Doubleday & Company, Inc., 1948.

Shaw, Arnold. *Belafonte.* Philadelphia: Chilton Company, 1960.

Spaeth, Sigmund. *History of Popular Music.* New York: Random House, Inc., 1948.

Stearns, Marshall W. *The Story of Jazz.* (*New American Library*) New York: Oxford University Press, 1956.

Wells, Evelyn Kendrick. *The Ballad Tree.* New York: The Ronald Press Company, 1950.

Wilgus, D. K. *Anglo-American Folksong Scholarship Since 1898.* New Brunswick: Rutgers University Press, 1959.

Index

Tennessee Ernie, 145
Terry, Sonny, 120, 143, 153
"This Land Is Your Land," 76
Tide, 128-129
Tin Pan Alley, 96, 97
"Tisket a Tasket, A," 31
"Tom Dooley," 107, 143, 207-208
Tomlinson, Ralph, 88
"traditional song," definition of, 10
Travis, Merle, 145
Treasury of Western Folklore, 34
"Tsena," 113
"Tubby the Tuba," 29

"Uncle Sam's Farm," 35
"Union Maid, The," 8
Untermeyer, Louis, 185

Variety, 93-94
"Venezuela," 12, 72
Vermont Folk Songs and Ballads, 77
Village Vanguard, 110, 144

"Wabash Cannonball, The," 51
Walton. *See* Sturgis and Walton.
Warner, Frank, 106, 120, 143, 153, 207, 208
Warren, General Joseph, 12, 189
Washington Square, riot in, 168-170
"Wayfaring Stranger, The," 33; radio show, 78
"We Gather Together," 38

Weavers, The, 10, 80, 105-121, 122-123, 134, 137-138, 140, 143, 146, 147, 154, 162, 224-225
Wells, Evelyn Kendrick, 50
Wendell, Barrett, 64-65, 66
Werber, Frank, 147
"When I First Came to This Land," 209-210
"When Johnny Comes Marching Home," 96
"Where Have All The Flowers Gone?" 230
"Which Side Are You On?" 124-125
Whiskeyhill Singers, The, 148
White, Cool, 31, 90
White, Joshua, 75, 79, 81, 110, 111, 120, 126
Williams, Hank, 115
Wilson, Earl, 105
"Wimoweh," 57, 112, 116
Woltman, Frederick, 123
Wood, Hally, 120, 146
Work, Craig, 144
Work, Henry C., 6-7, 92
"Wreck of the Old '97, The," 92
Wyman, Loraine, 68

"Yankee Doodle," 5-6, 13, 53
"Yankee's Return from Camp, The," 5
Yarbrough, Glenn, 149
"Year of Jubilo, The," 6-7
Young, Israel, 167